Legalities Of Love

Published by Blue Café Books
Morrow, GA 30260

Printed in the United States of America

Copyright © Carla F. Du Pont, 2006
All rights reserved

Cover art by Adam Tarmy

No portion of this work may be reproduced, stored in or introduced into a retrieval system or transmitted, in any form, or by any means (electric, mechanical, photocopying, recording or otherwise) without the prior written permission of both the copyright owner and the above publisher of this book.

This is a work of fiction. Names, characters, places, and incidents either are the products of the author's imagination or are used fictitiously, and any resemblance to actual persons, living or dead, business establishments, events or locales, is entirely coincidental.

I would like to express my sincere appreciation to…
Nacirema Williams
Constance Poitier
Thomas Huger III
Carmen Mason
Johnetta Washington

www.bluecafebooks.com

Chapter 1

When Yvonne discovered she was pregnant, she wanted to find the perfect way to tell her husband that she was carrying their first child. They had not been necessarily trying to conceive, but they were married and he made more than enough money to support them both. She knew that Victor would be excited, possibly even more than her.

She tried to think of all kinds of ways to introduce him to the idea that he was going to be a father. She could just come out and tell him, but that would be boring to her. Yvonne toyed with the idea of just not saying anything and letting the bulge of her belly show. By the time her stomach would have distended, the secret would have absolutely killed her.

Finally, the idea came to her. She settled on sending a card to his job. That way, his response was immediate and she would not be forced to wait forever to share in her joy. It was not long before she found the perfect card with the perfect saying. Yvonne was a woman on a mission.

Victor had been a divorce lawyer to the privileged for six years at Bowles and Laughton. Although his specialty was divorces, Bowles and Laughton delved in almost every aspect of the law.

The mail cart strolled down the hallway, guided by a young, high school graduate with bushy sideburns and curly brown hair pulled back into a ponytail. He never said much, just delivered the mail and moved on.

"Mrs. Balken, I told you not to worry. You'll get alimony. We are seeking for $20,000 each month and healthcare benefits," Victor reported to one of his clients.

The mail boy walked into Victor's open office door and set a single envelope on his desk, tipped his head and left.

"Yes...yes...yes ma'am. I think we can get you another, let's say, $5,000 a month." Victor turned half of his attention to the only piece of mail that he received. He immediately recognized the handwriting.

"Alright, Mrs. Balken, I will call you as soon as I get the details on the that." Before Mrs. Balken could give her closing salutation, Victor was opening his mail. Yvonne periodically sent him little love notes to his job. He suspected this was another. He loved getting things from her, the unexpected added such a flair.

He put down the phone receiver and tore into the mint green envelope. On the cover there were two bears, one grown up holding a baby bear in the air. The outside read *I have no doubt in my mind* and the inside continued, *that you will be the best Papa Bear you can be. Congratulations!*

Victor leaned back in his plush leather chair. He closed the card and read it again completely. On the inside of the card, the grown-up bear was cuddling the smaller bear in it's arms. He started smiling, figuring his beloved wife was trying to hint at something.

"Yvonne Russell, this is Victor Russell Attorney-At-Law. How are you doing today?"

"Very well, Mr. Russell. What can I do for you?" They often played this game. They were very much in love and every one knew it. They simply glowed when they saw each other and could not go a day without talking several times.

"My office received some mail from your residence and I am a bit confused." He stroked his pristine goatee. Victor had very sharp features that were accented by his warm brown skin. He was a bit taller than average and his build was slender. But Victor Russell was immaculate.

"What is there to be confused about, sir?" Yvonne was beaming on the other end. She knew that even though he may not have gotten what she was trying to say, she was only seconds from revealing her pregnancy.

"Okay Baby, for real. What is this card supposed to mean? I think you are trying to tell me that you really want a child and you think I will be a good dad."

"Close, but no cigar."

"Well, Yvonne, the only other thing it can mean is that you're…"

"Yes!" She was bursting at the seams and could not wait to get it out.

"You're pregnant?"

"Yes," she said this time a little more calmly.

"Oh my gosh! I'm gonna be a daddy!" Victor shouted jumping out of his chair. His secretary looked up and peered into his office. His voice was resounding.

"Yes, yes, yes!"

"When did you find out? How far along are you? It better be a boy!"

"Whatever, I found out last week and I'm about six weeks along."

"Oh, Baby. I'm so happy! We have to go celebrate! I'm coming home right now!"

"Baby, finish dealing with your young, rich, spoiled ex-wives club. I'll be here all day. I have no houses to show."

"I'm on my way home!" He said excitedly and hung up the phone before she could protest again. He knew Yvonne all too well.

She was sitting at her desk in the office of their house finishing up some paper work. She was a real estate agent, a profession that had really begun to take off for people in the metro Atlanta area in the past few years. After high school, she had no idea what she wanted to do and worked a host of dead end jobs until she almost tripped into real estate.

Yvonne found it to be a lucrative business for herself. She had charisma and a hunger to succeed. She primarily worked from her home office. She went into the main office once or twice a week. There really was no need to ever go in. Everything she needed was at her house, except for her super's signature.

She simply loved the idea of becoming a mother. Being 29, she felt that she had waited long enough and money was not a worry. She could do very limited work, or she could not work at all until she got ready to return. Yvonne had been smart and saved her money from the time she begun at 21 up until now. She always felt that she had to protect herself. In the fledgling job market, employment was unpredictable and so was selling big homes, expensive homes and receiving commission.

Real estate is not a salaried job and guaranteed nothing. You sell, you eat and keep your job. On the contrary if you do not sell, you suffer the consequences. She knew that her parade could be rained on at any time. Yvonne had money tucked away in a Roth IRA, invested in stocks and mutual funds and then an emergency cash, on hand savings.

All this knowledge did not come on her own. The day that she went to the real estate office to apply for a job, she had no idea what she was getting into. She waltzed her pretty self into the office. The secretary asked her if she had

Legalities of Love

a license, Yvonne pulled out her driver's license. The secretary laughed at her. The owner of the business, Mary Louise Parker, was standing there talking to the secretary when Yvonne approached.

"Do you know anything about real estate?" Mrs. Parker asked her straightway.

"Not really aside from the fact that I can dress nicely every day and make some good money." Mrs. Parker took a look at the young lady standing in front of her. She was not in a business suit, but rather slacks and a button down, which was fine. Her shoes were heeled open toe sandals, her hair and make-up were very conservative.

"What kind of work do you do?" Mrs. Parker probed.

"I work for the movie theater full time and part time at the community college switch board."

"Why do you have two jobs? Do you have any children?"

"I have to make ends meet. That's why I'm here." Mrs. Parker could see the look on Yvonne's face as she spoke. She invited the young lady into her office and closed the door.

Mrs. Parker began by telling Yvonne about her life. Being the senior lady, Mrs. Parker knew that if she opened up and told Yvonne about her past, that she could probably coax a true story out of Yvonne. Mary Louise started by telling Yvonne that she was introduced to real estate by her ex-husband. She joked that it was the only thing that he had given her. Well, that and lots of orgasms.

Mr. Parker owned a real estate agency and let his loving wife be his secretary. Mary Louise urged him to teach her the ropes and help her get a license. He never would, saying that there was no time for that. Her job was to answer the phone. She was always last on his mind. There were always open houses, home closings and clients to serve. It was not long before he started sleeping with one of his clients.

"The way that the story was told to me," Mary Louise thought back, "he was showing her the house and he started describing what an asset the fireplace would be to her life and things got hot and heavy. Needless to say, they had sex on the floor in front of the fireplace for the next couple of years until she felt the need to come clean."

"What do you mean she?" Yvonne asked.

"She, as in his affair. She was tired of sharing him and knew that it would be easier for him to leave me if I was filled in on what was going on."

"Did her plan work?"

"Yep," Mary Louise leaned back in her chair. "He figured after I knew about it, the painful part was over and he could just leave. He left me without a dime to my name. His mother should have taught him that you can't keep a good girl down. It took me years to recoup, but I've built quite a nice business here." Her arms were outstretched indicating her surroundings.

"Wow."

"Ten years after he left me penniless and heartbroken, he came crawling back to me asking me for a job. I wish I had a camera to take a picture of his pitiful face right at that moment." Mary Louise was laughing. She rubbed the back of her closely shaven do. Her hair was very short but spunky. The frameless glasses she wore made her look very sharp.

"No he didn't," Yvonne had her hand over her mouth. The woman sitting before her was very polished and had no reason to lie. Her dress was professional, as was the environment. Yvonne could not understand why this lady whom she had never met before was pouring out her sorted past. But it sure was interesting.

"First he asked me for forgiveness. After I would not take him back, he told me the truth." She said smugly.

"Which was..."

"Well," Mary Louise looked at Yvonne out of the corner of her eye. "His client, turned lover, had left him for another man and took him for everything. She transferred funds and went on vacation to Europe with her new lover to close out my ex-husband's hidden accounts. Accounts I never knew he had. By the time he knew what happened, she was rolling in *his* dough."

"That's what he gets."

"Yeah, that is the way things go. You can't just treat people a certain way and live life like it's not going to come back to you. It always comes back. Always. In one way or another. If you dig one ditch, you better dig two. So, tell me about yourself." Mary Louise prompted.

Yvonne proceeded to tell Mary Louise the story of how her mother was on drugs and could not choose her child over her high. Yvonne had grown up in the hood, but wanted so much more out of life. All of her friends were into the same things, drinking, smoking and partying. Unlike them, she was forced to take on a more adult role. Yvonne was more focused on being able to keep her lights on than getting a weekly hairdo. Going to the supermarket with food stamps was imminently embarrassing to her. That was not what she had planned for her life.

Even though she was young, she recognized that the life she was living was a cycle. Yvonne was determined to end it. Her mother was so high all the time, she did not care if Yvonne went to school or what she did. Growing up, she lacked having that maternal nudge. There was no nudge for greatness, no encouragement to do better.

Yvonne got a job at the local fast food joint. She told Mary Louise how she worked hard going to high school and working to keep food on the table for them. Her mother said she appreciated her daughter, but never showed it. The entire household became dependent upon whether or not Yvonne went to work. Her mother started stealing things from the house that Yvonne spent her hard earned money on.

The young girl would come home and find clothes and small appliances missing. She knew her mother was turning it all over for drug money. Forget stashing money in the house. If it was within those walls, her mother would find it. Weary from basically having to fight everyday for survival, Yvonne got a place of her own. The only thing she took with her was her clothes and she began a new life.

Mary Louise respected her ambition, even if it was just to have a decent job to make an honest living. She asked Yvonne where her mother was now. Yvonne confirmed that she did not know. Her eyes watered as she told Mary Louise that it pained her too much to see her mother like that. For a while, she would go visit her mother, but all Yvonne ever got was badgering for leaving her mother out there in the projects.

She knew that if she wanted to have a better life, she was going to have to leave her friends and mother behind. As bad as it was, she made a painful decision leaving the only life she knew, but at night, she could sleep knowing that she was more than likely not going to be robbed. The food in her fridge would not be bartered for drugs.

Mary Louise really saw the potential in the young woman in front of her. Almost two hours later, Yvonne emerged with a smile and a promise. After sharing their life stories with each other, Yvonne promised that she would start saving and studying for her real estate class. Mrs. Parker promised Yvonne a job at her office when the license was earned. One year later, after scraping pennies to get the class and the test, Mrs. Parker kept her word and Yvonne had a job literally the next day.

Seeing how much effort Yvonne had put into becoming a real estate agent, Mrs. Parker took the girl under her wing and taught tools of the trade. Yvonne was extremely thankful and stayed in the office from open to close everyday hoping to get sales. Mrs. Parker loved the fire that she saw in Yvonne and really gave her a push on good leads.

Mrs. Parker was the one who taught Yvonne about securing her future. She knew that if Yvonne got excited about the amount of money she was suddenly making, that it would be gone before she knew it. Mrs. Parker taught Yvonne all about diversification of funds and more importantly, not depending on a man.

Yvonne learned her lesson very well and had enough money put away even before marrying Victor not to have to work for a solid year or two if she chose. Victor added even more security to the equation. His clients were either women who felt betrayed by their husbands' jobs and affairs or men trying to keep their loving, faithful wives from recovering financial damages as a result of a failed marriage. Which ever the case, his clients were prepared to pay a hefty sum to get what they wanted.

Normally, it would be those very same clients who clouded his mind on the commute home concerned with ways to keep them happy and financially secure. This day was different. He was so excited. It was the perfect time to have a child. Yvonne had already expressed her desire to remain at home with the children until they were old enough to go to school. Victor had absolutely no quandary with that situation. He loved Yvonne for the stable family life she provided.

He was an orphan himself. He never knew his mother or father. His life had been filled with shuffling from foster home to foster home. He vowed to himself everyday growing up that he was going to be a lawyer and never have to want again. He only chose becoming a lawyer because aside from doctors, lawyers seemed the most prosperous. Victor could not shoot for the gusto of becoming Dr. Russell because the sight of blood irked him.

Having left his job early, he did not encounter much of the traffic that had become such a standard part of Atlanta city life. With no traffic, his drive was about 45 minutes. With traffic, the possibilities were endless. Regular rush hour traffic paces along at a speed slower than average, accident traffic inches along the highway.

Prior to marrying Yvonne, his apartment was a lot closer to the law firm. Yvonne wanted a nice home and community in which to raise their offspring. Fayetteville was the city that they chose. On the days that he did not have to be in court, he went in to work as early as 6 a.m. to avoid battling the 9 to 5ers. His was just another plight in the struggle to maintain good employment and have decent housing in the metro Atlanta area.

Traffic was easy moving now, around 3 in the afternoon. Thoughts consumed him and before he knew it, he was flying down Hwy 85 catching all green lights. It was like God himself was in on it. He saw his turn coming up and began to get a stir in the pit of his stomach. He did not imagine that he would be wound up so fast. It was not long before he turned on the street where he resided with his wife and now baby to be.

With the crescendo of every engine increasing toward her home, Yvonne's anxiety thickened. Every minute, she hoped her husband would be racing through the door. Finally, she heard the car door slam in the driveway and realized that a smile was on her face. Her husband really had come home.

"Baby!" Victor shouted. He did not see her, but he knew that she was home because her black Lexus ES was sitting in the driveway. He ran into the living room which had a view of the kitchen, nook and formal dining room.

"Baaa-beee!" He sang out again. Now he was on course to the stairs. He ran straight for their bedroom and she was not there either. He checked each of the 3 guest bedrooms. He was puzzled, he could not find Yvonne. As he took a mental inventory of all the rooms in the house, he realized he ran right past the office down stairs.

"Hey Baby," Victor said laying eyes on his beautiful wife. She was comfortable working at home. Yvonne's hair was dark brown and her complexion was the color of butter. She, too, was well manicured from head to toe. Both of The Russells had to look the part.

"Well, hello."

"You had me concerned when I could not find you."

"Unlike you," Yvonne started, "I actually work."

"Come here, girl." He grabbed her by the hand and propelled her towards him.

"Victor, I told you not to leave your job."

"Ok, you must be crazy. My wife went through the trouble of planning how she was going to tell me that she was pregnant and you think that I am going to stay at my desk filing motions and going through financial statements? Ha! That's not going to happen."

"I love you," Yvonne said.

"I love you, too." The two stood there, she was being held in a close embrace and Victor then leaned in for a kiss. Yvonne wrapped her arms around the back of his neck as they stood in the office in their embrace. The only sound that could be heard was their lips smacking on each other.

"Baby, no Juniors, okay?" Yvonne pulled away to say. Victor nodded his head smiling and pulled her back into him. He wanted to savor the enthusiasm. The novelty would only be like this once.

"Yvonne, we have to celebrate."

"Ok...what do you have in mind?"

"I don't know, whatever you want."

"Hmm," Yvonne breathed, "if I had known that you were really coming home, I would have gotten dressed and been ready to go out."

"Well, it won't take long. Go get ready," Victor egged her on.

"How can I get ready when I don't know where we're going. Actually, I'm fine in what I have on," Yvonne looked down at her jeans and casual button down. Victor looked down at her.

"It sounds like you obviously have something in mind."

"Yes, I do. Let's go to Union City," suggested Yvonne.

"There's nothing in Union City but car dealerships."

"I know, but I figured that since I am carrying your child that you might be ready to take my auto game to the next level."

"Auto game?" Victor repeated making fun of her.

"I told you I wanted a new car."

"Yvonne..."

"What? We are in a happy marriage, we are pregnant, we have a 401k, mutual funds and a house that has gained $100,000 in market value in 3 years. I think that we can afford a new car."

"Yvonne, your car is only 4 years old."

"Old, that's right."

"Where do you want to go eat," Victor asked laughing.

"I want a Lexus RX 300, Cherry red," Victor started to walk away, "...with beige interior and wood accents," she followed him.

He turned around to face her and told her that he was going to pick the restaurant and that he would think about her automobile proposal. That was enough to pacify Yvonne. She accepted his petition and grabbed her purse before walking out to his car to enjoy the evening with her husband.

They decided to go out for Japanese. Yvonne loved the fact that they cooked the food right in front of her and it was hot and fresh. She was too old to really care about all of the fancy food tricks that the chefs did before, during and after each show. They spent time talking and bonding. As usual, Victor shared stories about his crazy clients, scared their country club memberships would be cancelled or they would not be able to afford the latest hobo from Chanel. Yvonne talked briefly about her uneventful day and wanted eagerly to hear more about husbands trying to get out cheap.

Hearing about his job was almost as addictive as a soap opera. The difference was that the characters and the stories were real. There was no script, no storyline, just real life drama. Victor knew that his wife enjoyed hearing about his stories, although he never revealed their names. He would start with, "I have this lady..."

Then talk turned to whether or not the child was a boy or a girl. Yvonne just wanted a healthy baby. Victor was a bit more opinionated. If it was a girl, he wanted her in ballet or piano lessons. If it was a boy, his child was going to be put into little league as young as the system allowed.

Yvonne's imagination took her to years in the future with driving, college graduation and guessing possible occupations. Her husband told her she was getting beside herself, but he was happy that she was happy. He was even more endeared at the way that she exposed the truth to him. With it being their first child, they would experience all of those firsts together.

After the dinner, the Russells battled a bit of rush hour traffic to get home. Victor and Yvonne changed into more comfortable clothes and settled into the living room.

"I really am glad about this child," Victor put his hand on his wife's still unchanged belly. Their eyes fastened and she saw the sincerity in his soul. They began to kiss and he laid her down on the throw blanket that rested on the couch. Victor knew how turned on his wife got when he grazed her body lightly with his fingers. He took off all of her clothes and traced her body with his fingertips.

He gently let his hands run across every inch of her unchanged body. Innocently, she looked at her husband. She loved him more than anything else. Victor's very touch sent chills up her spine. Loving him was all she needed.

She yielded herself to him while basking in the radiance of his affection. He parted her legs and lay down between them. Yvonne was ready for what she knew was about to happen. He felt around for the moist consign between his body and hers. When he found it, he introduced himself to her. She sucked air in through her clenched teeth until he was completely inside.

He moved slowly, deliberately to a passionate beat that only they could hear. As he moved in and out of her, Yvonne wrapped herself tightly around him. She was so wet that the movement was easy for him. Victor could tell that his wife was close to climax by the way that her moans increased. He knew that he could let go himself. They reached their height together and lay together holding each other tightly.

Victor was walking to his car and his cell phone started to ring. Having a briefcase in one hand, his suit jacket and keys in the other, it was hard for him to answer it right away. He settled into the car and pulled out his phone to see who it was calling him. He figured that it was another one of his clients with a not so emergent emergency. His caller ID showed the name Crenshaw. 1 missed call. He took a deep breath and called the number back. He had a very long day in court.

"Victor, what took you so damn long to call me back? I've been calling you all day long. You act like you can just pick me up and put me down whenever you feel. I am not your little puppet okay? My name is not Yvonne," the young lady blasted into her receiver.

"Calm down, Monique! Leave Yvonne out of this. I've been in court all day, but you know that because Ms. Betsy said you left five messages!"

"Well Mister Big Shot Lawyer, if you got my messages, why didn't you bother to call me back?"

"I was focusing on my case," Victor was getting defensive, she could hear it in his voice. He was thinking about how his wife would have never called him acting so belligerent and accusatory. He never could figure out why he tolerated such behavior, but he was glued to her.

"I *am* your case! I am bigger than all of your cases! Did you just forget about poor little Monique?"

"No, I could never forget about you," Victor's voice softened. "I just wanted to keep my mind clear for the proceedings. You know how important that is."

"Victor I really needed to talk to you, though. Didn't you suspect that something was wrong since I was blowing you up all day?"

"I knew that if you were well enough to call, you were okay," he said halfway laughing.

"Well, I have something to tell you that is not a laughing matter."

"Monique, what is it now?" Victor suspected that she was pulling his leg. He was sitting in the car with the ignition running.

"I'm pregnant." Her voice softened.

"What?"

"You heard me Victor, I'm pregnant!"

"Get outta here."

"I am dead serious."

"Be honest, you are just saying that because I told you Yvonne was pregnant last week. You want to get in on part of the action."

"No, Victor, I am pregnant. There is no joke in this. Do you think I would joke about being pregnant to a married man?"

"Monique...you're pregnant...from me?" He was asking in disbelief. He felt his world begin to crumble.

"Yes."

"I'll call you back."

"For what? What good is that going to do?" She kicked it back into high gear.

"I need time to think...I mean, I... let me call you back Nique!"

"Victor you are not getting off the phone with me," Monique said forcefully. She could hear him exhale through the phone.

"Monique, I will call you later!" And the connection was lost. Victor just sat there in the parking lot. The A/C was blowing on high aimed right at his face. He pulled down his visor and opened the mirror. He just looked at himself. *How could I be so stupid? How could I have let this go so far? How could my other woman be pregnant?*

He knew that Yvonne was not going to stand for any of this. He could not believe that Monique was pregnant with his baby. This could not be happening. No, Monique was just jealous of Yvonne being pregnant and now getting all of his attention. She was starting to really feel her role. Monique knew way too much. She could destroy everything. She already almost did.

What if she was really pregnant? What if...? What if...? He thought back to the beginning.

Chapter 2

Victor saw her as she was standing in the atrium of the Bowles and Laughton Law Offices. She was a dark brown sundae. Her two piece skirt suit was navy blue. But the first thing that he noticed was the not so conservative length of her mid thigh length skirt. With the blazer unbuttoned, he had a clear view of her crème button down decorated with navy pin stripes. Her crème shoes matched perfectly, she left the collar of the shirt to lay over the collar of her blazer.

Ten seconds, he thought and he would be there. He licked his lips as he got closer to where she was standing. She popped her neck, parted her lips and exhaled lightly. *Two seconds, don't walk away, I'll save you.* He lengthened his last steps.

"Let me help you with that," Victor volunteered trying not to sound winded. The young lady's concentration was steadfastly on the marquee boasting lawyers' names and office numbers.

"No, thank you. I'm okay," she said without diverting her attention.

"Really, I work here and since you are looking for a lawyer, I'd like to introduce myself. I can tell that we are on the same page by your choice to dress like me." It was then that she turned her interest to the man that was speaking.

"Yes and I see that you are already full of hot air," she offered. Her smile was easy. The man standing before her was wearing a navy blue pinstripe suit.

"C'mon now, all I said was let me help you and you did not want me to. I had to say something to lighten the mood."

"What mood?"

"Just look around," he spoke softer, "at the stern faces. All of the ladies are wearing clothes made of the same material that my suit is and they don't give or flow. The colors are dark. The mood is so somber that once you step foot inside those huge glass doors you cannot tell the clients from the employees. Clients are worried about protecting their lives, their freedom or their standard of living. The lawyers are concerned with keeping a winning record." Taking it all in, her smile widened.

"I guess."

"So, instead of staring at all these foreign names, let me help you save some time."

"Crenshaw, Monique Crenshaw." She extended her hand.

"Victor Russell, Attorney-At-Law," he could appreciate how firm her handshake was. She took him in. From his tapered hairline edge to his perfectly tailored suit, cocoa brown attaché case, he was a work of art. Other than a thin mustache, he had no facial hair or a trace that there ever was. She could tell that he took very good care of himself.

"Nice to meet you Mr. Russell."

"No, the pleasure is mine. Now, tell me what type of lawyer are you seeking?"

"Divorce," she said recognizing his name from the marquee.

"Well, I'm the man for you. Let's go up to my office," he said while leaning in to press the 'UP' arrow for the elevator. She just smiled again and clutched her portfolio. Her teeth were bleach while against her dark tone. Perfect.

"Actually, I am here to see Dennis Sutton."

"Oh, well, its on the same floor." Victor tried not to show that he was taken aback. He was disappointed that he possibly would not get to make further acquaintance.

"My interview is in forty minutes and I wanted to make sure that I did not get caught in traffic. You know how downtown Atlanta is." Ding! The elevator doors opened and they stepped on.

"What position are you applying for?" Dennis Sutton was the office manager for the entire firm. His office just so happened to be located on the same floor as the divorce lawyers.

"Paralegal. I want to be in divorce law, I think."

"You think?"

"It's not as exciting as criminal law," Monique said as if it was obvious.

"That depends on who you ask. Personally, I love divorce law. I sure don't have to worry about putting people in prison and hoping that while they sit behind cold steel bars, they don't take me doing my job personally. Something had to make you consider divorce law."

"I was pretty much thinking along the same lines." Ding! They arrived at their floor walking leisurely from the elevator.

"You had the right picture," Victor encouraged.

"I just want to get my hands wet," Monique replied. "What I like most about this firm is that it is such a large firm. There are several different avenues of law for me to experience. I hope to find a home here."

"So do I. If I can be of any assistance, feel free to give me a call. As a matter of fact, stop by my office on your way out." Victor pointed her in the direction of the floor secretary, Ms. Betsy, and watched her walk away. Monique knew that he was standing there watching the ride of her hips as she swayed toward the desk. Even from the back, she was impressive.

Her clothes fit her very neatly. She tastefully revealed her coke bottle shape and managed to look very professional. Her hair was rather long, hanging down to about her mid back, though he was sure that it was not all hers. It still looked good. While talking to her, he also noticed how clean her make-up was even with splashes of color. Monique Crenshaw was a sight to behold.

After he stood in the corridor and drooled over her, he made his way to his office. His morning routine was always the same. He played his car stereo loudly to get amped up. Once at the building, he spoke to the main floor concierge, his floor secretary and ate a small breakfast at his desk. By small, his breakfast often consisted of fruit, granola bar or a bagel and orange juice or milk. Very predictable.

Today, the difference was he got delayed getting the ball rolling past the main floor concierge. Monique caught his attention. He felt that it was well deserved. Now he had to shake her off of his mind in order to have a semblance of a decent day. *I didn't even give her my card*, he thought. The truth of the matter was, he really did not need to have any form of a relationship with her at all.

Even if they did develop a relationship, it could be one of business at best. That would still be a great temptation. Monique, in that short period of time, had turned him on from the bottom of his soul. Sitting at his desk staring at his computer screen, he prayed that she would stop by on her way out.

"Victor," Ms. Betsy called over the speakerphone.

"Ma'am?"

"I have an urgent message for you."

"Urgent? The day just started."

"Victor," she said again with the tone of a mother. He knew what that meant. He was supposed to present himself front and center at her desk.

"Ms. Betsy."

"This young lady called you first thing this morning. She was the only call I've had so far," Ms. Betsy said referencing how early it was. She handed him a message memo.

"Thank you."

"Sure, I missed my 'good morning' from you today."

"Yeah, ah, I'm sorry. Good morning," he blasted trying to make up for his flub. He had his mind on something else, it truly had been a good morning.

"Oh forget it," she shooed him away.

"Could you please do me a favor Ms. Betsy?"

"What is it?" She always made it seem like he was asking so much of her.

"Tell me when that young lady leaves Dennis' office."

"You mean the young lady that you stood in the hallway talking to for ten minutes?"

"Ms. Betsy."

"What, you did? If she's visiting Dennis, what do you want with her?"

"Ms. Betsy."

"Alright, alright. Now go call your client before she has a coronary." Finally pleased, Victor headed back to his office. He called his client back and hurried their conversation. He did not want Monique to come by his office and think that he was too busy to talk to her. Time passed by quickly and before he knew it, Monique was standing at his door. She tapped and he stood up offering her a seat.

"How did your interview go?"

"It went well. He was pretty straight forward," she commented about Dennis' interviewing style.

"Yeah, he's like that about everything. What did he say to you?"

"The same thing that they all say," she was playing him now, "that he has more interviews and he will be in touch. It did not sound very promising. I wish I had a connect on the inside."

"Let me see your resume," Victor extended his arm. She flipped open her portfolio and handed him one. He scanned over it quickly, not really knowing what Dennis would have been looking for.

"Well..." Monique sat there anxious for him to say something.

"It looks nice. Let me keep this."

"Why?"

"So I can take it to him. I'll tell him that I spoke with you and blah, blah, blah. I'll see what I can do."

"Thank you Victor," she squealed as if that was not the response that she was expecting from him. How could he resist her? She was sitting in front of him with her legs crossed and all he could see was legs for days. Her lip gloss shimmered every time she moved her lips. It was driving him insane. Victor knew that he had to get her out of there before he closed the door and had his way with her.

"No problem, Monique. I just want to help a sister out. I know how hard it is to get a job in Corporate

America, especially for us. We need to look out for each other."

"How is your day going so far?" She asked him smiling, showing her pearly whites.

"It's gotten off to a great start," he said holding a glance with her, "but I have a lot to do." She took the hint. Her job there was done anyway. Now he had the resume with a number to reach her should he choose.

"Again, it was nice meeting you," she stood up and smoothed her skirt. "I hope to hear from you soon." Victor stood up and shook her hand, then walked her to the door. He caught a deep breath and slowly walked back around to his desk. Then he remembered that he needed to talk to Dennis.

Victor walked into Dennis' office down the hall and closed the door behind him. He talked to Dennis about giving Monique a job and saying how he had briefly spoke to her without her knowing that he was an associate there. Victor was very smooth in embellishing the truth. He went on and on about her and how he thought that Monique would be an asset to Bowles and Laughton. Dennis informed Victor that he appreciated his comrade's input and would definitely consider hiring Monique for the position.

As the day progressed, he could not get her out of his mind. He kept picturing her smile, her lengthy legs and her sexy walk. Every other minute, he was glancing over at the resume that sat on the corner of his desk. Victor needed something to get his mind back where it was supposed to be.

He knew how to get himself more grounded. He picked up the phone to call his girlfriend. Yvonne would be able to give him a reason to do right by her. Plus, he figured that by talking to her, he could get in the right frame of mind.

Yvonne was glad to hear her man's voice. Anytime during the day, she could drop what she was doing for him, with the exception of showing a house of course. He knew how much she loved him. She let him know it every time she saw him, her face lit up, every time they spoke, he could hear it. He told her that he wanted to take a minute out of his day to just hear her voice and he could not wait until their respective days were over so he could see her. She shared his sentiment.

As Dennis was going through his interviewing process, Victor was determined to give him reminders about Monique. It was not enough to make Dennis suspicious, but it was not hard to figure out why Victor wanted to have Monique hired as a paralegal. She was beautiful and who would not want to have someone as good looking and as pleasant as her to work around?

Richard Worthy and Victor Russell were both divorce lawyers who worked on the same floor. They were about the same age, hired around the same time. It was natural for them to kind of stick together in their struggle to prove to the old heads that they could get the job done. The only difference was Richard was a step ahead, being white.

Richard was a yuppie if there ever was one. Everything about him was average except his salary and his personality, both of which he used to get women's attention. Once he was done with them, he threw them out with the day's trash and sought another challenge.

Although he knew he could not get involved with his own clients, there were a host of desperate, love deprived, divorcees coming to that floor. He had his pick of the litter. What made that situation even better was, most of them were on the rebound and they knew it. They did not want to jump right into another relationship, however relief from sexual tension was another thing. That is where Richard Worthy Attorney-At-Law stepped in.

Victor and his buddy Worthy sometimes went for drinks after work. They were both, for all intents and purposes, single. Victor had Yvonne, but no ring on his finger. Worthy had a slew of woman with no ring in sight.

The bar was a popular one, frequented by other lawyers, sometimes judges and officers. It was a lucrative watering hole downtown. Everybody had on suit and tie, very classy crowd. They would go to politic, buying rounds for other Bowles and Laughton attorneys.

Worthy and Victor would play a round or two of pool over the drinks of their choice. Victor would sit back and laugh as Worthy tried to schmooze fellow female lawyers. He would try to get Victor in on a piece of the action. Victor had more fun watching him than anything else. The next day without fail, Worthy would tell Victor all about his escapades.

It was no surprise when Monique was hired for the job. All of the guys wanted some fresh blood in the office and she more than fit the bill. She spent her first day being introduced to the staff and learning her way around. When she made it to Victor Russell's office, they embraced like old friends as he welcomed her to the firm. He told her that she owed him a lunch. Life could not have been better for the sexy little young paralegal. She could not wait to get off to tell her friend all about it.

"How was your first day on the job?" Alicia asked Monique.

"Girl, it was great. I knew he was going to look out."

"Who?"

"Victor, the real cute lawyer I met when I went on my interview. Remember, I told you about him."

"The one by the elevator," Alicia was reminding herself, "right. Yeah, he told you he would put in a good word for you."

"I guess he did, it sure helps to have someone on the inside," Monique bragged excitedly.

"I taught you well. What trick did you use to hook that fish?"

"I used no such thing." Monique rightly denied the accusation.

"You had to have done something. You don't get something for nothing, Nique. And I know you, you like to throw some bait out there to give you an advantage."

"For real Alicia, this time I didn't do anything," Monique smudged the truth.

"So, he just told you that he was going to put in a good word for you?"

"Yeah, cause he's my bro-tha, man!" Monique started laughing.

"That's alright. You better keep that one close. He may come in handy for us later."

"I think he definitely will come in handy for me. Girl, he is fine! And dresses nice, too."

"Nique, he's a lawyer! He's supposed to be nice." Alicia used the reference to his paycheck equaling how well kept he was.

"What I'm saying is, he is not the stuffy, Poindexter type. He has soul," Monique thought back and got an image in her head of Victor standing in front of the elevator.

"Let's hope his soul can get us another come up." Alicia joked.

"I hope to make a come up of my own." The tone in which Monique made her last comment sounded deviant. Alicia should know. She had been friends with Monique since high school. They were two years shy of their ten year high school reunion and it seemed that they spent the entire time together.

They did not miss a beat from the college parties, to each other's family cookouts. Alicia and Monique had been there for each other. While Monique took a lifetime on deciding to pursue a career in law, Alicia had been working photography for a while. She did mostly freelancing work, weddings, family photos or alternative senior pictures for those students who wanted to be different or could not afford the big guys. Recently, she had begun to do small time model portfolio pictures that were starting to bring in good money.

Being a freelancer, she created her own schedule which included free time. With such an unpredictable agenda, her love life was anything but normal. She could be involved with as many men as she could handle, they never knew when to expect her to be free.

While over the past eight years, she was gaining a bit of a reputation around Atlanta, she was still far from being able to just pick up and do for herself at her leisure. A few times during the past eight years, she had to get a 9 to 5 to pay the bills when photography was in the slumps. Her men were plentiful, her bills always paid and she was showered with gifts.

Monique thought it was funny to watch her friend work guys over, which is why she took mental notes. Alicia was so smooth about what she was doing and who she did it to. She was a manipulating machine. Things always worked out in her favor. She would be a confidant, a lover, a mother figure or whatever her men needed. Monique was often amazed at how many hats her friend wore. To Alicia, it was all in a day's work.

Monique felt the need to brag a bit about Victor. He was her best catch yet. She knew he was going to be her ace in the hole. She could not wait to get back to work to see his clean shaven face again. It would be several days before she would be able to see Victor again. His court schedule was tight. He had a few clients back to back who required all of his time and energy. Many times, when he was in his office, his door would be closed just to keep from being sidetracked. She began to crave seeing him again. She had to make the best of the split second moments that they would have in the hallway.

"Victor, I still owe you one," she called out as they were headed towards each other. She was going to the copy room, he was going to the conference room in the opposite direction.

"Owe me one?" Victor was a bit confused, his mind had been scattered over the last couple of days. Now, they were facing each other, stopped in the hallway.

"Yeah, lunch. I've been waiting. I always pay up," she said in a slyly seductive tone.

"How could I forget?" An innocent smile came to Victor's face.

"I don't know, but I don't want you to think that I was trying to get out of it easily."

"Monique, I have been extremely busy with these cases, but I can free up some time to eat. Talk to Ms. Betsy, she'll tell you what I like and meet me in my office at 2." He started back on his trek to the conference room.

"2?" Her voice showed disappointment as he was walking away.

"Sorry, late lunch today kiddo." Victor then turned and quickened his pace. As she was told, she went to Ms. Betsy and was given a choice of Victor's favorite delivery lunches. Ms. Betsy often had to order for him.

Like clock work, Monique showed up to his office and walked in the opened doorway. She had two plastic bags in one hand and a drink carrier in the other. Victor put his hand over the phone and whispered for her to sit down then went back to his conversation. She took off her peach suit jacket to get more comfortable, revealing her tight, white bodice.

"...yeah, Baby I know. That's good, that was a big sale...I'm proud of you, you worked hard...Tonight? Tonight is not good for me...Tomorrow, um, you got it, I'm all yours...I love you too...Bye."

"Lunch is served," Monique said already taking the sandwiches out of the bag when he got off the phone.

"Ah, I had a feeling that you were going to order this." Victor excitedly clapped his hands together while on his way to close the door.

"Ms. Betsy said you had not had this in a while."

"No, I have not."

"Why did you close the door?" Monique questioned.

"If it makes you uncomfortable, I'll open it."

"No, I was just curious."

"This is my quiet time. When my door is closed, people know not to knock. Lunchtime is not work time."

"Look at your view," she complimented walking behind his desk to the rear wall which was a huge window. There was only a few feet between the desk and picturesque scenery.

"It's not the corner office."

"But it's an office. You're already a few steps ahead of me." Victor swiveled his chair to face the beautiful woman standing beside him. Even though he had just gotten off of the phone with his girlfriend, the eye candy in front of him was amazing. She donned another skirt suit, this time a light, girly peach. It made her skin simply glow. Monique wasted no time adding life to her building. She had a floral hair scarf wrapped around the front of her head letting her long hair flow in giant curls down her back 70's style. Her off-white pumps further elongated her legs.

"You'll get there," he cheered.

"I may need a little help," she said and turned to face him.

"Believe me, you have a supportive staff here. We will all help you get where you want to go." Monique bent down to her knees in between his. She placed her hands on his thigh.

"I told you that I always pay up."

"Monique I have a girlfriend…"

"Oh, you mean the one you were just on the phone with? I'm not worried about her. She can't compete with me. I want you, Victor. I always get what I want." By the time she was done talking, his zipper was down and she was massaging him with her hands.

"See, its not so bad is it? Just relax," Monique coaxed.

"But..." Victor started to talk but she was already seducing him orally. He felt like he should stop her, but he did not really want to. She was so spontaneous and bold. He was falling in love with her. She continued to work her magic on him, knowing that the door was closed but not locked and someone could walk in at any time. Victor sat there as she effortlessly pleased him. The last thing on his mind was finishing lunch or his endearing girlfriend. His breathing got shallow and unsteady.

"Umm...umm," she hummed only loud enough for his ears to perceive. It produced a mild vibration in her mouth that he could feel. The only lunch that Monique was devouring was a juicy forbidden fruit. It was quite a delightful substitute. He could see a passionate satisfaction in her eyes that only heightened his own excitement.

He was conscious not to let out any sounds. He kept licking his lips, trying to keep his composure. His hands were wrapped around the armrests of his chair. Victor could feel himself loosing the battle and for once, that was not such a bad thing. Monique was making love with her mouth and if it was love, he was falling hard. Finally, he exploded, mildly shaking in his chair. She arranged him the way she found him, without him comprehending what she was doing. He was riding on an invisible breeze. Monique stood up and smoothed her own clothes, picked up the bag with her lunch in it and walked toward the door.

"Now, I'm almost paid up." Victor opened one eye and looked at her puzzled. He thought she had more than paid her debt to him.

"Almost?" He whispered.

"I always finish what I start," she replied with one hand on the door and with that she left. Monique would have loved to stay and finish her lunch with him. By leaving after the deed was done, she was making more of a statement.

That was the beginning. Victor knew right then that he should have put his foot down and made it clear that there could be nothing between them. He did not and Monique began treating him periodically. They made sure to keep things discreet...around the work place. Alicia knew blow for blow what was going on.

"Nique, I can't believe you did that to him. At his job?!" Alicia screamed across the living room to her best friend. Alicia had her hand over her mouth in disbelief.

"Our job," Monique corrected her.

"What has gotten into you? I am so, so, I don't know! You ought to be ashamed of yourself!" Alicia laughed at the gall of her friend.

"I am, but I can see the look in his eyes. He needs me."

"Needs you? Didn't you say that he has a girlfriend?"

"How serious can they be if he's letting me do all that?"

"They could still be very serious. You are throwing yourself at the poor man. It's not like he was coming on to you."

"He was trying to play hard to get."

"You should have let him play and left it at that."

"When did you get so self-righteous?" Monique questioned her friend.

"Ok, ok, just be careful. You know how that situation can get." Alicia warned.

Chapter 3

If there was a grain of sand for every time Victor thought about Monique, he could have made a beach. She had proven herself to be an imminent distraction from his relationship with Yvonne. Leaving Yvonne was never on his list of things to do, as a matter of fact, it was quite the opposite. He just knew that he was stuck between two women who cared deeply for him, one was in the form of love and the other, lust.

The workplace affair was beginning to take place everywhere, especially the workplace. They were sneaking out to movies and dinner. More commonly at work or Monique's place. Since Yvonne was so trusting, if he told her that he had to stay late to work on a case, she believed him when he told her, particularly since on the rare occasion when she called him to momentarily give him a break at work and he answered the phone. Unbeknownst to her, he was usually having an after work romp right there in the office.

Monique knew exactly what was going on and felt very proud of herself having put such a rift between Victor and his lady. She was pulling rank and even though she was not number one, she felt that she was more than just a roll in the sack. Victor's feelings for her were impossible to hide. His whole countenance changed when he saw her. It was becoming increasingly difficult to bury their extracurricular activities from their comrades at work.

Victor was in a serious relationship and they both stood to loose their jobs should the news come out. The truth of the matter was, the level of passion that stood between them was impossible to deny. Keeping what was at stake in the back of their minds, Monique still managed to maintain an intensity that kept him coming back. Her adventurous sense of sexual exploration amazed him. She was so bold. That was what he loved about her.

His favorite jaunt was in the conference room. Victor had an end of the day meeting in the conference room. Most of the firm was already gone for the day and Monique was looking to say good-bye for the night.

"How did you find me?" Victor asked a bit surprised when Monique walked in the door of the conference room. Victor was collecting the presentation props he used during the meeting.

"C'mon Babe, it wasn't hard. The meeting was on the board." She responded seductively. The conference room had to be reserved in advance and no one was permitted in or out unless the door was open. The blinds were always pulled closed.

"Well yeah, you're right. How was your day today?"

"My day was filled with thinking about when I was going to get a chance to see you."

"Aww, that's so sweet," they shared a warm embrace. "What are you doing tonight?"

"You."

"I won't be able to pull any thing today."

"Why not? I haven't had a piece of you in a week?" She pouted and poked her bottom lip out.

"Yvonne and I have plans." His tone was very straight and to the point. Despite knowing that she could not hold a light to his girlfriend, it still irked her to be reminded of such.

"What kind of plans?"

"It doesn't matter, does it? I have to go." He said not rushed, but definitive.

"Victor...I really miss you. I miss us."

"Nique, I miss you too, but tonight I just can't do it."

"Victor," she began twirling his tie, "why don't you make a couple minutes for me?" She suggested.

"Nique, I have to go," he pleaded. "My meeting ran over and Yvonne is..." Monique pulled him over to her by the tie and planted a delicious kiss on him. He did not stop her, he rarely did. She took her free hand and rubbed his manhood through his pants. It was already where she needed it to be. He was pulsating against her hand.

"Just a few minutes," she whispered into his ear. He barely nodded his head in approval, once again under her spell. She gently tugged on his ear lobe while walking him over to the table. When she felt that she reached the table, she slid her rump on it. He was kissing her fully now. Their tongues were exploring every part of each other's mouths.

She zipped down his pants and freed him while at the same time he pushed up her dress. There was no denying the heat that was between them when he entered her. They both felt it and it was driving her wild. Monique knew that she was Victor's weak spot. He would put anything on hold to get a piece of her. What was really getting her off was the fact that Yvonne was probably sitting at her house staring at her watch while Monique was having sex with Victor on the conference table.

Anyone could have easily strolled into the room and caught an eye full of what was going on. The awareness of their bold actions propelled them to a higher threshold of passion. Monique was panting heavily, careful not to be louder than a murmur for fear of being found out. She arched her back as her shared lover thrust harder and harder. At last, she reached her pinnacle and pushed an unsatisfied Victor away from her.

"Thank you," she said before he could even catch his footing. She slid off the table just as easily as she slid on.

"That's it?"

"Yeah, thanks."

"Oh, so you just used me?"

"You use me to fulfill the urges that your girlfriend isn't capable of."

"I'm not done," Victor replied and turned her around against the table to finish what she started. With her back to him, Victor felt around for where he previously was. She was sopping wet. Once he found it, he immediately persisted to pleasure himself. He had already done his job to quickly finish off Monique's waning.

"Victor," breathlessly escaped her lips. No sooner than she mouthed those words, he withdrew himself and grabbed on to the table for support. Now, they were both satisfied.

Victor proceeded with his plans to take his girlfriend out. It was not hard to compare the differences between the two. Yvonne's idea of romantic was a quiet candle lit dinner. Monique thought romantic was high heels, fishnet stockings and a Fredrick's get-up. Spontaneous to Yvonne was making out in the movie theater. Monique took impulse to a whole new level. She would lift up her skirt in a heartbeat for Victor in the office supply closet.

When he pictured himself with a house, children and a wife, spontaneity gave way to family life. Yvonne just fit the bill. He felt that Monique's behavior was a bit over the top and too risqué. The last thing that he wanted was for the kids to see their mother in a compromised position. Yvonne did not give him the most exciting love life, but she was an awesome homemaker and great mother material. She allowed him his space and she was quite successful in her profession. Yvonne did not depend on her man.

Monique would often bring up small things she wanted or places she hoped to visit. It took her some time to get comfortable enough to ask him for anything. Unlike her competitor, Yvonne would simply share with Victor the things that she had gotten herself rather than hint around until he felt like buying. He liked Yvonne's initiative.

Attitude was a whole new consideration. Yvonne was easy going. She rarely got upset and could control her temper. Monique let him know when he let her down. She whined to get a reaction from him. Sometimes she would burst into his office, close the door and complain on and on about not seeing him. He could not bare the mental picture of dealing with Monique and all she brought to the table for the long haul.

After carrying on an affair with Monique for almost a year, Victor decided to tell her that he was moving on with his life. He knew that she was not going to take it easily, but that was not his concern. He was also well aware of the temptation that he was to face should he break things off with her. Monique was no girl off the street, a one night stand that he would not have to deal with. She held a position, not only at his firm, but on his floor. Even if he did not want to see her, he had to. 'No' was not a word that she was used to hearing. She made that clear in the beginning. He just needed to find the right time to tell her it was over.

Monique and Victor were having lunch in his office as they did on a number of occasions. Victor was checking his interoffice email. Worthy sent him a note about grabbing drinks after work. He had a case deserving of a celebration. One of the other paralegals walked past his office. He could not help but notice the clean baby blue Coach bag that was draped over her shoulder. What really caught his eye was the color.

"Mary, come back!" He called out. Mary turned around and stuck her head inside the door.

"Yes, Victor. I will be done with the briefs in two more days." She said flinging her hair to the side.

"No, I was going to comment on your purse."

"Oh," she said blushing, "thank you so much. I just got it."

"Who makes that?"

"Coach, do you really like it?" She asked squinting her face begging for his approval.

"Why don't you do me a favor and buy one for my girlfriend. She would love that." He was giving her the ultimate sign of approval.

"Sure."

"I need something else to go with it though."

"They have other accessories in this color," Mary began. "They have belts, scarves, key chains and wallets."

"How about a scarf. Oh and a belt."

"Alright." She agreed and put her hand out for Victor's credit card. Once she got it, Mary started back down the hallway.

"What about me?" Monique asked in a quiet voice, her eyes pleading.

"Hey Mary!" He called out again. Mary backtracked, sticking her head in the doorway again. This time, she said nothing, just looked at him. "What other colors do they have?"

"Black, red, orange and cream." She looked up in the air trying to picture the store's set up.

"Get me a cream one also."

"With a scarf and belt as well?"

"Yes, thanks." Mary walked away from his office with her instructions. Monique silently clapped her hands together. Another victory. The next day, Victor called her into his office. She was hoping that her new accessory ensemble had arrived.

"I have something that I believe you requested." He said slyly to her.

"I believe that you do," she responded seeing two white bags on the floor. The clue was the word 'Coach' in a box in black typing on the bag.

"You know that I can't give it to you here. That will be just begging to leak our business out into the firm."

"So when do I get it?" She wanted the bottom line.

"I'll drop it by your place after work."

"Ooh, fruit salad." Monique said walking closer to his desk, he was having his morning snack.

"Made fresh last night." Monique helped herself to a freshly cut square of pineapple.

"This is so sweet," she said with a mouth full. "Where do you buy your fruit?"

"Yvonne made it." Soon as the words escaped his lips, she spit out the half chewed pineapple into her hand.

"Monique, was that necessary?" She deposited the fruity remains into a piece of printer paper and threw it in the trash.

"I'll see you at my place," with that she walked out of the door. Victor thought her reaction was funny. There was no reason for her to behave that way. True to his word, after he got off, he drove directly to Monique's apartment.

When she opened the door he presented her with the bag that she had been craving to peer into. Monique pulled him in by his tie. She tore into the bag to make sure that all she was expecting was inside.

"Aren't you going to thank me?" Victor said.

"Give me a minute, dang," she laughed. Taking the bag into her bedroom, Monique poured the contents out on the bed. There was the hobo bag, the matching scarf and belt. She tied her long weave up into a loose ponytail with the scarf and proceeded to take off all of her clothes. She clasped the belt around her waist and slung the purse over her shoulder. Using the full length mirror in her room, she checked herself out and then walked into the living room.

"Now that's what I'm talking about," Victor commented rubbing his hands together.

"I wanted you to see what your money was spent on." She said seductively before giving him a mini walk down the 'runway'.

"Do I need to pull out some dollar bills?" He joked, feeling himself get aroused by what he saw standing before him.

"No need. I'm going to put some clothes back on." She scurried back towards the bedroom. Victor jumped up and ran behind her. He caught up with her just as soon as she reached the door. He took the purse off her shoulder and dropped it on the ground, kissing her.

She responded back by kissing him on the lips and unbuttoning his shirt. He walked her over to the bed and she led herself onto it. Weightlessly on top of her, he maneuvered his pants off. The non spoken language between their lips was hot and torrid. It seemed that they could not get enough of each other.

"Give it to me," she whispered in his ear. He knew exactly what that meant. Her legs were already in the assumed position. The access was easy. Besides, he knew the terrain, he had been there before.

There was no love to be made. Victor thrusted inside of her like he was in a race for a prize. The only runners in the race were Monique and Victor. She loved his animalistic sense. He was so primal when she needed to him be, or soft when she craved their sex to last. Using his hands to support himself, he moved up and down. Monique ran her fingers down the deep crease in his back. Damn that man was fine!

As she moaned, he was not satisfied, he needed more from her. He slid his hands under her back until he reached the cheeks of her buttocks. He spread them apart, sending him deeper into her. She yelled out. That was what he was after. They were both feeling it now.

"Big Vic! Big Vic!" Her chorus gave him the stamina to give her what she was looking for. He knew how to please a woman and Monique was no different. There were two more sessions after the first. When it was all over, he lay there recuperating.

"Why don't you stay with me tonight?" She asked, knowing that she was trudging unsure territory.

"I can't."

"Why not?" Monique was laying on her side facing Victor, he was fixed on his back staring at the ceiling.

"I have a girlfriend."

"And?"

"She calls me in the mornings or spends the night at my house. I can't stay here with you."

"Yes you can. Call her and tell her that you're still at the office and its going to be a long night."

"What do I say when she calls my house in the morning and I don't answer?"

"Beat her to the punch, call her before she calls you. I just don't want to spend the night alone. Please," Monique begged. In her efforts to get her beau to spend the night with her, she ran him away faster. Victor lay there thinking, *this girl is really desperate.*

If she had not brought up his girlfriend, he would not have left. Thinking about the wrongdoing that he had just participated in, prompted him to put on his clothes and leave. Monique was upset at herself for even saying anything. Maybe if she had not said anything, he would have fallen asleep. In his defense, he did lay it down and she was exhausted. He had already delivered two gifts, the Coach ensemble and the gift of himself.

"Hey Russell, how's it going?" Victor's co-worker popped his head into his office. They called each other by their last names.

"Hey Worthy, haven't seen you in a while," Victor responded to Richard Worthy.

"Yeah I know, where have you been?"

"Worthy, I've been right here."

"Man, every time I stop by your office, the door is closed or the board has you in court. You are working too hard."

"Working too hard? Is there such a thing?"

"C'mon dude," Worthy said rolling his head from side to side, "we have people to do the dirty work for you. Let them do it."

"People to do our dirty work?" Victor Russell laughed at his comrade.

"Yeah, you know, those cute paras. Tell me you have seen Monique today. That sista got it goin' on!" Victor laughed at Richard trying to portray his afro centric side.

"You've been looking at her?" Victor knew Richard was pretty cool as far as guys at the office went, but he always remained professional.

"Don't play righteous with me brotha. She is gorgeous! And thick too! Boy, I'd like to get a piece of that." They both laughed.

"Worthy, you can't be serious."

"Yes I am. Her ass looks so good in that pant suit today. I would love to give her some work." He danced rhythmlessly in the chair.

"Wow," Victor started to get uncomfortable and readjusted in his chair. He could not tell if Richard knew something and was trying to let him know or if he was simply in adoration of Monique. Either way, this was not a conversation that he wanted to have right now.

"I know that you only have eyes for Yvonne, but don't skip out on the eye candy dude. That sista is hot! You can put her to work for you."

"I already have," Victor said..

"You already have?"

"Not like that... I gave her some research on a few of my cases." Victor was quick to correct himself.

"Ahh man, dude. You are the man! You devil you."

"No, Worthy, I..." Victor just started laughing.

"Yes you did. How was it? Was it good?" Richard crawled to the edge of his seat across the desk from Victor's chair. He was waiting on the scoop of the year.

"You know Bowles and Laughton frowns on interoffice affairs," Victor reiterated to his friend.

"Who the hell cares? We are talking about you getting it on with Monique."

"There is nothing to talk about," Victor said.

"I knew she had the hots for you. You're the only brotha on this floor. Damn! I would have loved to have a taste of that," Worthy stood up.

"Keep your head on straight," Victor advised.

"Yeah. You go home and get a break from the office sometime. I'll catch up with you later dude," Richard walked out. Victor was totally confused by the whole conversation that had just happened. Richard was stepping a bit out of character. Sure, every time that Richard had a new intimate interest, he made it known. Occasionally, there was a problem letting the crazies go, but he rarely got straight to the point like that. All he talked about was Monique. *Oh well,* Victor thought brushing it off and turned back to face his computer.

"Victor," Ms. Betsy's shrill voice exploded over the speakerphone.

"Yes mother," he mocked.

"Your presence is requested in the conference room." No sooner than he heard the words, his mind raced back to the last time that he was in the conference room. That was a favorite for both he and Monique.

"What's going on, I didn't get a memo," he picked up the receiver.

"Well, Senior Bowles requested that you be there." They all referred to the partner as Senior Bowles since his son also worked there.

"Ms. Betsy, something's up and you know exactly what it is."

"I sure do, but it's not my place to tell you."

"C'mon..." his urging usually worked.

"Ok, ok," she started whispering in the phone, "Senior is going to announce his retirement, now go on."

"I'm there!" Victor hung up the phone and straightened his tie. He skipped down the hallway. The floor was never loud, but it was always busy. He noticed that he did not hear anything or see anyone milling around. He figured he was the last person to be called into the conference room. He opened the door and everybody yelled, *Congratulations*!! The shout was followed by applause. Victor was standing there with his mouth wide open, then he saw Yvonne approaching him.

"Baby?" Victor said extending his arms toward her.

"It's an engagement party!" Senior Bowles shouted. He was a hearty old man with a head full of gray hair and a belly that proved how prosperous his firm was. "I heard that you finally asked this young lady to marry you and I decided to throw you an engagement brunch!" Victor shook hands with the grinning head honcho.

"Where's Ms. Betsy? I know she had something to do with this."

"Here I am," Ms. Betsy came walking from behind him. He gave her a big hug and kiss. Ms. Betsy had a sweet heart. She loved keeping the environment light and celebratory as often as possible.

"Well everybody, after we get a speech from the guest of honor, then we can all dig in," Senior Bowles said.

"What can I say?" Victor stammered overwhelmed by what was happening.

"Tell us we're awesome dude. Yeah!" Richard Worthy yelled from the back of the room and began clapping for his own idea while everybody else just laughed. Victor figured that Worthy had been his distraction.

"You got me, you really got me. I can't believe that somebody didn't slip up and mention it. Especially, Dennis, we all know he can't hold water."

"Yeah, we didn't clue him in until this morning," Ms. Betsy noted.

"Thank you, all of you, for helping me to celebrate this special progression in my life. This really means a lot to us," he was holding Yvonne's hand. "Starting tomorrow, there will be a money tree in my office and..."

"Let's eat!" Senior Bowles bellowed cutting Victor off. He ran to the front of the line. Since he was the boss, no one argued with that.

"Baby, how long did you know about this?" Victor looked into his fiancée's eyes as he spoke to her.

"For about a week. Ms. Betsy called me."

"I can't believe that you didn't tell me either."

"Why would I ruin your surprise?"

"Congrats!" Yvonne stepped back so that Victor could get well wishes by the other lawyers and paralegals on the floor. There were probably about 40 people packed into the conference room. There was a spread of doughnuts, muffins, fruit, juices and finger sandwiches.

Yvonne knew many of his coworkers since they had been dating for so long. She had been to her share of company functions. She thought it was a nice gesture of his company to throw such an event. Even though it was not a big deal, the fact still remained that they took the time to assemble the floor and throw a small celebration.

After mingling, Yvonne and her beau went to his office and finished their plates. They were laughing and joking. For the next hour, they chatted about everything under the sun. Yvonne told him that she was going to have something special for him when he got off work.

On the other side of the office, Monique was having a fit. She had finally seen her rival in the flesh. Victor had a picture of the two of them on his desk. Other than that, Monique never had the ironic pleasure of laying eyes on her. Yvonne was well presented. Her hair was lengthy and real. She was a couple shades lighter than Victor and quite attractive. Her build was relatively slender. Monique was a few inches shorter and well stacked.

It was hard for Monique to keep from running over to her saying something, anything. She was two seconds from introducing herself practically the entire time Yvonne was in the conference room. *Did you know that I had sex with your fiancée on this very table about ten times?* Monique had to hold herself back. She could see why Victor was holding on to her. She was very modest and seemed like the wholesome, motherly type. To Monique, the girl did not look like she had a bit of freak in her. Still, she thought, she was a better catch.

She had a few words that were on her chest that she needed to get off. She figured that this was as good a time as any. She rapped on Victor's office door knowing that on the other side was a loving couple, whose fun she was about to ruin. Of course, unsuspecting, he answered the door and his face lit up in surprise.

"What are you doing here?" He asked.

"Is that the way you greet me now? It used to be with a kiss." She responded walking past him.

"Monique," he called out to her as she walked past him. "Monique!" He called out into the office in vain.

"My name is Monique," she extended her hand to Yvonne who was sitting on Victor's couch. Yvonne felt very uncomfortable. From the moment that Victor opened the door, he was behaving oddly. She was not sure why.

"Who are you?" Yvonne asked puzzled.

"I am Victor's lover. I know all about you."

"Victor's lover?" Yvonne asked wanting to make sure that she heard the lady correctly. Victor raced over to where they were.

"Victor?" Monique questioned him.

"Baby," he turned to his girlfriend Yvonne, "this is a paralegal from my office."

"Yeah," Monique chimed in, "I know all about how he has sex with me because you can't keep him satisfied."

"Baby," he started to talk over Monique, "this girl is crazy! She has a crush on me and I told her there could be nothing between us because I am dedicated to you." Yvonne moved back from Victor's grasp and started to cry. Victor called out to her and she simply ran out of the door.

Monique knew that image in her head would never play out in a million years. Although she did not want to let him go, she knew better than to mess up his relationship with Yvonne. If that was her only plan to get him, it would sabotage what she had with him and the battle would be lost anyway. Pushing Victor away from her was not ever what she had in mind.

In her heart of hearts, the attraction between she and Victor was purely sexual. The sex was so good and so wild that she began to fall in love with him. He never painted a picture for her that gave her any idea that things could go any further. In her mind though, as soon as Yvonne messed up the relationship that she and Victor shared, Monique would step up to the plate.

After waiting nearly a year, quite the opposite had happened. The false sense of security that she had was hers and hers alone. Now, he had decided to take his life to the next level with someone else and she still had to face him at work from day to day.

"Victor, we need to talk." Monique started this time in the flesh instead of in her mind.

"I don't like your tone Nique," he responded. He had been having such a good day. Now, he sensed that it was all about to change.

"I don't like the way that you handle your business."

"What are you talking about?"

"How the hell are you going to propose to her?"

"What do you mean, how am I going to propose to her? She's my lady." His words were sharp and his pitch was innocent.

"Victor, we had something going. You just up and proposed to her without telling me," her voice had turned into a high pitched squeal.

"Since when do I have to tell you about the things that I decide to do with my life?"

"Don't you think it would have been nice of you to let me know what was going on before I heard it in the street? If it weren't for the little party, I wouldn't have even known you were engaged."

"You would have found out eventually."

"You are sleeping with me. I think I have a right to know."

"I never said anything to you about taking this, whatever it is, any further than what it is…"

"But…"

"Shut up! Let me finish," he had to be rash with her, something he never had to be with his girlfriend. "So what if we slept together. What does that mean? My heart is with Yvonne."

"You can't be serious," Monique said rolling her eyes. Even though they were trying hard to keep the conversation below earshot of their cohorts, there was no mistaking the anger within those office walls.

"Yes, I love Yvonne," Victor was speaking of his girlfriend.

"How much do you love her? The last time that I saw you, you had your pants down rolling your little love handle around in my mouth."

"Nique, Nique, don't be so…"

"Don't 'Nique' me! I have been there for you. I love you, Victor. How could you do this to me?"

"You do not love me," he said blowing her off, "you are in lust!"

"Well, I lust you and you lust me!" She was trying to plead a case and he started laughing at her. Her allegorical way of expressing herself tickled him. Monique was standing in front of his desk with her hands tucked on the waist of her hour glass figure.

"You knew what the deal was when all of this started. I told you from the very beginning that I had a girlfriend."

"You also let me come between the two of you. You never cared about staying at work a few extra minutes to spend time with me or going to the movie every now and then." The debate had become a full fledged argument.

"What's ten minutes when I can spend the rest of the night with Yvonne?" He knew the words would sear her, but he had to do what he had to do.

"Yvonne this, Yvonne that. Now you want to call her by her name." Victor's personalizing his girlfriend was eating Monique up inside. Her mind kept going back to the conference room and seeing the copasthetic look on Yvonne's face.

"Ok Nique, this is all irrelevant. I love her and that's all there is to it."

"Victor, how could you do this to me?" Her whispers were low, but powerful. Her animosity became unmistakable. Victor was sitting in his office chair while she leaned over his desk.

"How could you leave me?"

"Leave you? Monique I was never with you! My heart has always been with Yvonne."

"She can never do for you like I do."

"Monique, don't fool yourself," he chuckled. "I love her and this is where it ends."

"So it's not enough for you to pull the wool over my eyes, but you want to throw this all away too?"

"There is nothing here, Monique. We had sex, good sex, hell even great sex and that is it!" Victor put power behind his statement. "If you are going to have this reaction to me making strides in my life, then we need to let this relationship go."

"You are willing to just walk away from all this?" She asked with her arms outstretched.

"All what?"

"On the couch in your office, on the floor…"

"Nique..."

"...in the supply closet, in the bathroom..."

"Nique..."

"...on the back porch, in the movies..."

"Nique..."

"...on your desk, on the counter..."

"Nique, what are you trying to prove?"

"I'm trying to tell you that I am the best. I am the one you need to be choosing if you have to choose. I should be the one that you want to share the rest of your life with."

"Why, because we have a good sex life?"

"We have an awesome, incredible, fantastic sex life."

"And you know what? That's all it is. There is no substance." Victor stood up and headed to the door.

"I won't let you leave me," she started towards him. He opened the door and stood silent until she found her way to the other side.

It became pretty apparent that he was not being considerate of her feelings. She felt so hurt. How could Victor plan to spend the rest of his life with a woman that he was not faithful to? Why did he decide to do this now instead of a long time ago leaving Monique to scrape up her feelings? She had so many unanswered questions.

In her silence, she came to the revelation it was up to her to put things back the way she felt they needed to be. Victor was expecting her to just wallow away in pity and be too ashamed to have any further dealings with him. He had no idea who he had been sleeping with.

A couple days passed before Monique conjured up the courage to go speak with him. She replayed the scenario in her head repeatedly. Knowing that she would be struggling with her words, her goal was simply to let him know that she had no intention of letting him go that easily, if at all. At last she decided that practicing was going to make her sound rehearsed. She just wanted to go and get her feelings off her chest.

"Victor, may I have a word with you?"

"Sure Monique," he granted her wish. What other choice did he have? She was standing in his office, not on the phone or email.

"I've been thinking," she closed the door behind her knowing it would give them more privacy. "I really miss having you in my life." She pranced over to his desk in an all black skirt suit. As usual, the jacket button was undone revealing her black and white laced camisole top.

"I'm engaged," his response to her was hard and cold. She made her way around the desk and sat atop it. She neglected to cross her legs.

"I know, but like I said, I miss you. I was not a total distraction to you. I don't understand why you want to cut me off." Sitting down, her skirt came almost as high as her mid thigh. Victor had a clear view of what he was missing.

"You were a distraction to my relationship," he said attempting not to look under her skirt.

"I never made any demands on you, Victor," her tone was very soft. "I never asked you to leave her. I was happy with the time that you gave me. That was always enough for me. I was perfectly aware that there was someone far more important in your life than I was. Yet, that never bothered me." She lied.

Victor leaned back in his chair looking at her. Here was the woman he had been having an interoffice affair with. There was so much for them both to loose. He could loose his job if anyone found out and be hard pressed to get another one. Who would he use at Bowles and Laughton as a referral? She could loose her shot at the experience she was trying so hard to get. It would be a lot easier for her to move on.

Then there was Yvonne. He had just asked her to spend the rest of her life with him. She would be heartbroken if she found out Victor had another woman on the side. Monique's sculpted legs dangling from the top of his desk made it hard for him to think of anything else. In his mind, the last thing that he wanted to do was succumb to her, however, his body was already in another place.

"What...ahem," he had to clear his throat, "what do you want from me Monique?"

"Big Vic, I want things to go back to the way they were," she slipped off the desk and took one step to the window. She put her black pump in the window sill and started slowly pulling up her skirt. Victor felt around in the back of the top drawer for some protection and joined her in an upward stance.

He did not want to do what he was about to do, but felt powerless to stop it. The tension between them was the same as it had always been. Strong. There was almost no turning back at this point. The damage had been done and he was weak in her seduction. She was so sly, like a mosquito. By the time her presence was felt, he had been bitten.

Monique had won another battle. She left Victor wondering, *how did I get myself back into this? This girl told me that she was not leaving even though I'm engaged and I fell for her, again.* He was very angry with himself. He knew it was going to take more than a solitary effort to pry her off of him.

"Victor, I need to see you in my office," Dennis Sutton paged via speakerphone.

"Dennis, I can't right now."

"You can and you will. Right now," Dennis demanded. Victor, disgruntled, let out a deep sigh and proceeded into the office. He was stunned to find Senior Bowles and Monique in the office as well.

"Close the door son," Senior said.

"Okay Victor, it has been brought to our attention that you are having an affair with Monique here," Dennis got straight to the point. "You did know that was against policy, right?"

"Yes," Victor replied. He was so embarrassed. Lying, that the affair never happened was his first instinct. But Monique was sitting in the chair next to Senior Bowles, so they already knew the truth.

"I love having you around here, you do good work Victor." Senior Bowles took over. "Your clients rave about you. We carefully filtered through hundreds of applicants before offering you this job. It will be a shame if we have to let you go. Now, let this serve as a warning. If I hear anything else about you and this young lady or anybody else in this firm, there will be no more discussion." The entire time that Senior Bowles was talking, not once did he even acknowledge Monique.

"I do apologize Senior Bowles for letting you down. The decisions that I made were not in the best character. I will not let you," he nodded his head towards Senior Bowles first then to Dennis, "or you down." It was clear to Monique the meeting was between the boys.

"Alright Victor, get back to work." Victor left Dennis' office and headed straight for Richard Worthy's office. He rushed inside and slammed both hands on Richard's desk.

"Dude, what is your freaking problem?" Richard pushed himself away from the desk to put some space between Victor's face and his.

"You ratted me out to Dennis."

"Huh?"

"About Monique, don't play with me."

"Hey man, that had nothing to do with me."

"Like hell it didn't. You went on your own assumptions and tried to get me fired." Victor's face was contorted in such a way that it had Richard scared. He had never seen Victor like that. The black man was coming out.

"You let it out, Victor. You make your bed, you lie in it," Richard said smugly and began to snicker.

"That's messed up. Don't ever come to me for anything, ever!" Victor walked out of Richard's office knowing that he had just lost an ally.

Chapter 4

Victor was walking to his car and his cell phone started to ring. Having a briefcase in one hand, his suit jacket and keys in the other, it was hard for him to answer it right away. He settled into the car and pulled out his phone to see who it was calling him. He figured that it was another one of his clients with a not so emergent emergency. His caller ID showed the name Crenshaw. 1 missed call. He took a deep breath and called the number back. He had a very long day in court.

"Victor, what took you so damn long to call me back? I've been calling you all day long. You act like you can just pick me up and put me down whenever you feel. I am not your little puppet okay, my name is not Yvonne," the young lady blasted into her receiver.

"Calm down, Monique! Leave Yvonne out of this. I've been in court all day, but you know that because Ms. Betsy said you left five messages!"

"Well Mister Big Shot Lawyer, if you got my messages, why didn't you bother to call me back?"

"I was focusing on my case," Victor was getting defensive, she could hear it in his voice. He was thinking about how his wife would have never called him acting so belligerent and accusatory. He never could figure out why he tolerated such behavior, but he was glued to her.

"I *am* your case! I am bigger than all of your cases! Did you just forget about poor little Monique?"

"No, I could never forget about you," Victor's voice softened. "I just wanted to keep my mind clear for the proceedings. You know how important that is."

"Victor I really needed to talk to you, though. Didn't you suspect that something was wrong since I was blowing you up all day?"

"I knew that if you were well enough to call, you were okay," he said halfway laughing.

"Well, I have something to tell you that is not a laughing matter."

"Monique, what is it now?" Victor suspected that she was pulling his leg. He was sitting in the car with the ignition.

"I'm pregnant." Her voice softened as well.

"What?"

"You heard me Victor, I'm pregnant!"

"Get outta here."

"I am dead serious."

"Be honest, you are just saying that because I told you Yvonne was pregnant last week. You want to get in on part of the action."

"No, Victor, I am pregnant. There is no joke in this. Do you think I would joke about being pregnant to a married man?"

"Monique...you're pregnant...from me?" He was asking in disbelief. He felt his world begin to crumble.

"Yes."

"I'll call you back."

"For what? What good is that going to do?" She kicked it back into high gear.

"I need time to think...I mean, I... let me call you back Nique!"

"Victor you are not getting off the phone with me," Monique said forcefully. She could hear him exhale through the phone.

"Monique, I will call you later," and the connection was lost. Victor just sat there in the parking lot. The A/C was blowing on high aimed right at his face. He pulled down his visor and opened the mirror. He just looked at himself. *How could I be so stupid? How could I have let this go so far? How could my other woman be pregnant?*

He knew that Yvonne was not going to stand for any of this. He could not believe that Monique was pregnant with his baby. This could not be happening. No, Monique was just jealous of Yvonne being pregnant and now getting all of his attention. She was starting to really feel her role. Monique knew way too much. She could destroy everything. She already almost did.

Things had changed dramatically since the beginning. Monique had turned from an inconspicuous naughty dessert into an almost daily, pilled high second plate. Shortly after Senior Bowles and Dennis Sutton found out about the affair, Monique was seeking new employment. It was good for Victor in the way that it removed the pressure of being caught, but then he had to go out of his way to see her. Her place was on his way home.

There was absolutely no way that he could face his wife after getting the news. He called her to say that he wanted to unwind and he would be home a little later. Yvonne told him not to eat, that she was going to be cooking and dinner would be served in two hours. His hide away spot was a bar half-way between the job and his home.

It was a small hole in the wall, bar and pool hall called Sparky's. He loved Sparky's because the lights were low, the bartender kept his cup full and nobody bothered anybody else. The awesome chicken wings and cheese sticks helped. The bartenders loved his tips. Victor loosened up his tie and walked right in.

"Another long day in court," her sweet, sultry voice sounded like someone was playing a harp when she spoke. No song was as good as the Sonya song. He had been going to Sparky's for years. She was more than just a bartender, she had become a confidant.

"I've had a day like you wouldn't believe," he replied in a low monotone voice.

"You know I'll take care of you, Victor," she handed him a double shot of Hennessy, "like nobody else can. Don't you forget it. Go ahead and lay it on me."

"Sonya, I don't want to burden you with my problems," Victor tried to brush her off before dusting the first shot.

"See that one," she pointed to a guy at the end of the bar with his head down, "he's a burden. He's in here every single day drinking himself into a stooper. Most of the time when you come down here, I already know it's about court. Today, you look worse than normal."

Sonya was short and brown skin. Her hair was twisted into short locks dyed red on the ends. They were just long enough to put into a short ponytail at the top, she let the dreds in the back hang at her nape. She was a thirty something year old lady with one child and he was her life. After school, she made sure that he came to Sparky's, which was only a block from their apartment, do his homework.

If he did not have homework, she made him study anyway. Sonya was determined not to let her son become another statistic. She was putting herself through college and he accompanied her to her night classes. Sonya had just had one bad break after another throughout life, but you could hardly guess it seeing her smile. Knowing how much she was struggling, Victor often helped her out here and there. He would go school shopping for her son, Timothy, clothes and supplies. Victor would give Timothy pocket change and give Sonya a few bucks to buy some grocery or cater herself.

Yvonne knew all about Sonya and Timothy, she met them in the beginning when she and Victor initially started dating. One of the things that she admired about Victor was that he was not too good to try to give someone else a helping hand. Timothy was twelve now and thanks to his mother, had a promising future. Victor knew that he could trust Sonya. What was said to her, stayed with her.

"I'm alright," he attempted to give her a weak smile, although it did not work.

"Victor, I'm going to take those folks' orders and when I get back, I want to know what is troubling you," there it was again. Her song. Every time he saw her, his mind ventured back to the time of the Harlem Renaissance when Black folks used to dress up and get clean to go to the club. The drag was the most popular dance and the ladies wore huge finger waves in their hair. All the guys had pocket watches with long strings that attached them. Inside the smoky club would be a jazz singer. That is who Sonya reminded him of. It was all in her voice.

"Monique is pregnant." Victor started on command as soon as Sonya got in front of him. She gasped as her mouth flung open. He told her about the whole situation. One thing that made him really want to open up to Sonya was the fact that she did not judge. Being a woman, she could sympathize with what Yvonne was going to go through if she ever found out that Victor had been cheating.

She never talked condescendingly to him or any of her patrons.

After the fourth shot, Victor requested a bottle of water. If he showed up home wasted, Yvonne would be on the hunt to find out why. Being plastered, he might blow his cover. Sonya did tell him that he had gotten himself into a doozy and he needed to figure out what he was going to do and fast. Victor decided it was time to head home and thanked Sonya for her ear. He paid for his drinks, his small order of wings and gave her $100 on her grocery. They hugged and she told him to be careful.

Victor had a ride ahead of him. He was so broken, he did not know if he would cry or scream when he laid eyes on his loving wife. He knew in his heart that Yvonne would never have done anything like this to him. He was beside himself. In his desperation, he came to the conclusion that Monique was going to have an abortion. She had no choice in the matter.

He was not going to willingly have an illegitimate child while he was married to someone else. He would set up something with Monique so they could talk. He was sure that she was not exactly pleased with the situation and she would want an easy out as well. In his mind everything seemed so simple, he just prayed that it would be.

When he arrived home, the aroma hit him. He walked in to see Yvonne putting the finishing touches on the salad. She was excited to see him, her face said it all. They greeted each other with a kiss. She immediately began fixing his bowl of salad to start the meal off. Knowing her husband the way that she did, she was sure he was starving.

"I have something for you," Yvonne said to him as he sat on the couch. He was trying to put on a brave face but that was going to be very hard for him to do looking her in the eyes.

"What do you mean?" He painfully added an inflection to his voice to try to hide the pain. His head was pounding. She could sense that his day had gone sour and appreciated that he was trying to hide it for her sake.

"Baby, part of being married is sharing your hurts, your aggravations and disappointments. I'm here if you want to get it off your chest," she gracefully petitioned.

"Thank you Baby, but I really don't want to talk about it." *I can't talk about it*, he thought.

"Ok, just remember what I said. I don't want to see you suffer. There should be a box on the floor next to the couch, open it." Victor recognized that she was sensitive to his needs. To reveal the source of his behavior would probably end their marriage on the spot.

He bent down to grab the box. As he opened it, he thought about how much Yvonne loved him and how much he knew he meant to her. He thought about how she did not deserve what he was putting her through. She was a good wife and had not, to his knowledge, wronged him. She always thought of him and put him first. She cooked most nights of the week and kept the house spotless. Their sex life was good and frequent.

Inside the box was a new attaché case. The one that he already had was used everyday, it had taken a beating. She thought that he could use something special. Yvonne loved giving Victor gifts just because. To her it added a little spice and flair to their marriage. She had it monogrammed with his initials.

"Baby, you didn't have to do this," Victor said getting up from the couch. He had given the case a full once over, inside and out.

"I wanted you to have this one. I ordered it last week. I am so tired of your other one. You need to chuck it. That old attaché case is done!" She exclaimed laughing. He gave her a hug and a kiss. She, in turn, handed him a bowl of salad and he saw what was for dinner.

"Oh, you spoil me so good!" He said realizing that he was smiling, genuinely, for the first time in several hours. It faded fast.

"Boy, go sit down, take the salad bowls and I will bring over the dinner plates." He did as he was told. Yvonne cooked shrimp scampi over fluffy fettuccine noodles in a butter wine sauce. Just a hint of garlic and spices made it all come together. Oh, it was so good! He absolutely loved it. His day was shaping up a bit better. He managed to keep his mind off of his illegitimate fetus long enough to shovel down a home cooked meal. They held a bit of conversation, but Yvonne could tell that he was distracted. Victor was determined to get the madness over with as soon as possible.

Bright and early the next day, Victor arose to the smell of breakfast cooking. Normally, his wife would prepare him something fast that he could eat while driving or a snack for work, if she fixed him anything. She felt that he needed some cheering. She made some scrambled eggs and grits, which he ate mixed up together along with a few links of sausage.

As soon as he got in the car, he was calling Monique. His morning commute was filled with anxiety and pressure. Pressure because he had no idea just what she had planned. Anxiety in the pit of his stomach told him that maybe she would be crazy enough to think that they could actually pull off having a child together. His stomach was queasy as the phone rang in his ear. They agreed to meet at her house the next day after work. He would leave the office in enough time to meet her at her house as soon as she got off. Thankfully, her work schedule was a lot more definitive than his.

At about 4:00, Victor turned off the ignition in her parking lot. He had beaten her there, but he knew not by much. All day, he rehearsed how he was going to break the news to her. He hoped that she felt the same way. By the time that he arrived at her house, he had convinced himself that he was going to be running the conversation. There was no way that Monique could not see things as he did. She would not want to risk ruining his life. He was already giving her what she wanted, a piece of him. This was just a complication that they could eliminate and move on with their lives, a little bit more carefully.

He was getting impatient. Every two minutes seemed like twenty. He repeatedly looked at the time in his dashboard. Victor started restlessly tapping on the steering wheel. He was mentally willing Monique to show up and fast. After unknowingly making him suffer for 15 minutes, she pulled into the parking spot next to him. She could see the worry on his face. He had not slept all night long. As they proceeded wordlessly into her apartment, he was thinking about when he attempted to terminate their relationship. That seemed like centuries ago.

"Okay, since you have had an eternity to think about whatever it is that you had to think about, what did you come up with?" Monique opened the conversation with a biting tongue. Victor knew that she was referring to him getting off the phone promptly after she told him that she was with child. She took off her lime green blazer and leaned back on the plush pillows of the couch. Her skin was a beautiful contrast against the light color of her suit.

"It was only one day and not even a full 24 hours." He was always defending his actions with her. She portrayed herself to be more of a wife than his own wife did.

"Whatever Victor," she said sitting across from him. He already found a seat while she put down her things. "You don't have to be slick with me. We have a problem."

"I have a solution." Even though he thought that his answer was the quick and painless one, his tone did not reveal any hope.

"It better be good." Her attitude towards him had completely soured in the last day. She hated to be put on the back burner.

"Your stank little 'tude needs to go."

"I'm pregnant or did you miss that on the phone before you swiftly hung up."

"Monique, let's cut through the chase and get it over with because this is a side of you that I just don't like."

"Yes let's."

"I think both of us agrees that this is not an optimal situation here."

"Right."

"And this could not have come at a worse time."

"Any time that this happened would have been a bad time." She seconded the motion.

"Okay, okay, Nique, you don't want to have this baby do you?"

"Come again?"

"I think we should have an abortion."

"We? Since when did this become a we?"

"Since we started making decisions together."

"When was that because I totally missed it?"

"When we started having an affair." Victor was being very frank with her.

"What you mean is, you think I should have an abortion. I know you won't go with me."

"I will if you want me to," he said aiming to be sensitive.

"Do you know how much that costs?"

"You know you won't have to worry about that. Listen, I think that…"

"Why is an abortion your first call to defense?"

"Nique, I'm married! You keep forgetting that!" He stood up and started pacing. The situation was making him very anxious.

"And you have a baby on the way." She added just in case he forgot about Yvonne's pregnancy. She was still bitter that she was not the one he chose.

"Is that what this is about?"

"No, but," Monique's added cleverly, "it is quite an ironic situation."

"Ironic hell! This is a horrible situation. I think you getting rid of this baby would help us to get back to normal."

"Normal, hmm, what is normal? Is normal you spreading yourself thin between me and your wife? Is normal telling me you love her too much to leave her but you still want an all access pass to my booty? Is normal leaving work early so that you can play in me before you go home to kiss her?"

"Enough!" Victor yelled, "enough. This is not an ideal circumstance for either one of us." He was wiping his sweaty palms on his suit pant.

"You're right, it's not. Maybe this child will be just what I need."

"What?" Victor asked in surprise. He stopped pacing and looked at her.

"At least this child will love me unconditionally."

"Nique that is the most ridiculous thing that I've ever heard. That is an awful reason to have a child."

"That way, I can have a piece of you with me at all times."

"Nique you are off your rocker," her temperament changed so fast. She went from being sore spirited to angry to needy. He could not get her and what was going on with her. He figured that since it was inside of her, she had grown somewhat attached.

"So *we* are going to have an abortion?" She asked for clarification.

"Yes *we* are. Let me know when the appointment is and we'll take it from there."

"So it's settled. I'll let you know."

"Alright, good." Victor stood up and kissed Monique on the forehead and walked out to his car.

Alicia and Monique had not been out in a while. They were usually good to see each other a few times a week. Monique had been so sick that it was all she could do to get to work everyday. Calling in had become routine. Alicia called to check on her everyday and finally decided to stop by. Monique had cracker wrappings all around the living room, they were one of the few things that she could eat and not get sick.

"Hey Mama," Alicia said hugging her friend when Monique answered the door.

"Hey," Monique was a tad weak.

"I'm sure that you have a year's supply of crackers, but I bought you some more. Oh, and some orange juice and soda. O. J. supplies folic acid and soda helps with nausea also."

"Thanks, put it in the kitchen."

"So what are we going to do about this?" Alicia asked her friend. The question sounded much like Victor a few days prior. Everything was about 'we'.

"Victor and I decided to have an abortion."

"An abortion?...Ok," Alicia was not at all shocked, Monique's presentation was what seemed odd. She figured that if anybody pushed for the pregnancy to be terminated, it would be him.

"What other choice do I have, Licia?"

"I did not say that I wasn't going to support you. In my opinion, even though you did not ask for it," Alicia joked, "I think that is probably the safer bet. Neither one of you is in a position to have a child."

"What is that supposed to mean?"

"Monique, in case you haven't noticed, you are sexing a married man! Married! I told you to leave him alone a long time ago. Did you really think that you were going to have a chance with him especially after he tried to call it quits with you after proposing?"

"Not really," Monique answered honestly.

"So why did you stay?"

"I don't know. I thought that I was in control of the situation."

"Til you realized that you were sprung, huh?" Alicia was trying to keep it real.

"He's sprung too," Monique spat out and started laughing.

"He's married. He has it in-house, he can get it whenever he wants. You, on the other hand, are waiting on him to call and arrange a visit. If you start holding out, believe me, he will not be going without."

"Obviously, she's not doing her job because he keeps me around."

"Does it make you proud of yourself to say that? You sound like an idiot! He's the one that's in control."

"How?"

"He tells you when he wants to see you, how long he can stay and now that you're pregnant from him, he is telling you what to do about it."

"Not necessarily, we both thought it was a good idea."

"Nique, you are really playing yourself. Who are you trying to convince here? I know he was the one who suggested it." Alicia was getting frustrated.

"So are you saying that I should keep it? Girl, if I keep this baby, I will have a true meal ticket. He's a lawyer so he knows that he'll have to pay child support."

"He also has friends who are judges and lawyers. Have you ever heard of scratch my back and I'll scratch yours?"

"No, think about it, I could truly make a come up. If he didn't pay child support, he would have to pay for my silence. So I'd get money either way."

"Come on, Nique. You can do so much better than him."

"Was your purpose coming here today trying to make me leave Victor?"

"I just hope that being in this predicament opens your eyes to show you how stupid you are being. You've been in this for almost 3 years now and it's not getting any better. Instead of him leaving his girlfriend, he married her!"

"I'm going to get this procedure done next week. I need a driver."

"Call his ass!" Alicia got up stormed out. She was too through with her friend. In all this time, Monique had not sought out anybody who was worth her time. In all actuality, she knew that Alicia was right about everything she said.

Monique knew that she really did need to move on. Victor was never going to leave his wife. If he did, it was going to be on his own accord or due to problems they were having, certainly not for Monique. No matter how hard she tried, she could not get his attention off of Yvonne. She kept trying to con Victor into spending the night or slipping up on his routine to give Yvonne something to suspect. It never worked. Victor was always on top of his game.

Despite the fact that Victor initially told her they were going to handle the situation together, ultimately she was left to do it on her own. He told her that he and Yvonne had plans. Monique was hurt and confused, the last thing she wanted to do was call Alicia. Monique cried for hours after she got off the phone with him. She understood everything that her friend was trying to tell her the week before was true. Victor did not care about her. He cared about protecting his lifestyle and his interests, neither of which included her.

Alicia reluctantly came to her aid and went to the clinic with her. Victor did, however, give her the money and a little bit extra to take herself shopping. To Monique, that was like a slap in the face. She could not believe that he reneged on his word. She was convinced that he did not fully understand the complexity of her pregnancy. In his mind, the abortion was going to take care of everything. He would have no more worries and once again, she would get the short end of the stick.

With Alicia being as outspoken as she was, it was hard for her to hold her tongue. 'I told you so,' was right on the verge of showing its ugly head. Monique's feelings were so bruised and it was evident. Her whole spirit seemed down as she stepped into her friend's car.

"Are you sure that you want to go through with this?" Alicia asked finally, the ride had been silent.

"Umm hmm," she nodded in affirmation. Monique was set on doing just what her lover instructed her to do.

"Cat got your tongue?"

"Umm hmm." Her mood was exceptionally somber. Alicia knew that Monique's heart was not in this procedure. Her job was not to judge or impose her opinion on Monique, but to support her. Alicia hoped that with the ending of this pregnancy, Monique and Victor's relationship would come to an end as well.

Monique wearily walked into the clinic with Alicia close behind her. Once inside, she filled out the necessary paperwork and handed her clipboard back to the nurse inside the window. She sat there thinking about what she was about to do. She was taking a life in her hands and that was not her job to do. To turn around now would mean that she did not keep her word. Her mind immediately went back to her conversation with Victor. *I think we should have an abortion...I think both of us agree that this is not an optimal situation here...Nique, I'm married...you keep forgetting that...let me know when the appointment is and we'll take it from there.*

There were a few other people in the waiting room with them. The first couple was clearly a mother and her young daughter. The girl appeared to be fast and was trying to grow up before her time. Her legs were crossed and she was bouncing the top leg up and down while popping her bubble gum. Her mom stared straight ahead, her face told the whole story. Sitting next to them was a couple who seemed to be in college. The guy was holding hands with the young lady to let her know that he was there to support her. She was resting her head on his shoulder. Then there was Alicia and Monique.

A nurse called Monique's name and she went into the doorway. The nurse took all her vitals and went over the paperwork on the clipboard. She described the process to Monique in mild detail and told her to feel free to ask any questions. The first step after all of the medical waivers were signed was the ultrasound, to assure that she was in fact pregnant.

"How far along am I?" Monique asked. The nurse tried to hurriedly print the ultrasound without Monique seeing it. Monique had already caught a glimpse of the black and white 2-D picture of what was growing inside her.

"I'm not a doctor, I can't really say."

"You can estimate, you do this every day."

"If I had to say, I would put you right at 10 to 11 weeks." The words hit her hard. She sat up. Before, she had not even heard the crinkle of her paper gown. The sound was now unbearable. She gradually slid off of the table, standing to her feet.

"I'm gonna go now," her words were barely audible.

"Ma'am?"

"I'm leaving." It was a bit louder this time. The nurse could tell that she was pained.

"I said that I was not a doctor, I could be wrong."

"You could be right," Monique countered. Her words were very calculated. The nurse looked at her as if something was clearly amiss. Monique was staring at the floor as she spoke. She appeared spaced out, like she was not there.

"Ma'am, if you don't want to go through with this, then don't." The nurse tried to be comforting to her.

"I don't. I will not give up my baby." Monique spoke in a monotone voice. The nurse continued to encourage her and instructed her to put her clothes back on.

When Monique reared her head around the door, Alicia was pleasantly surprised. There was no need to ask about what prompted her not to go through with it. Alicia knew that her friend did not want to abort that baby, even if she was not bringing it into the most desirable of circumstances. Victor had been the driving force through the entire thing.

While Monique had been forced to handle the situation on her own, the so called pressing plans that Victor could not escape from was taking Yvonne to the movies. They caught a matinee, so the crowd would not be bad and then had lunch at Yvonne's favorite restaurant, Gladys and Ron's Chicken and Waffles.

They enjoyed each other's company. Victor was in especially good spirits. As far as he knew, his problems were already over. Monique's appointment was early that morning and there was no reason to believe that he had not convinced her to go through with it. After movies and lunch, the couple went back home and enjoyed a lazy day around the house.

"Hello Rosemary," Yvonne waved to her neighbor. They both headed toward the median of their properties.

"Hello Yvonne, how are you?" Rosemary was a house wife. She had long, fiery red hair and skin that looked like porcelain. Her son looked nothing like her.

"Fine, looks like we are making progress." Yvonne spoke of the fifteen month old who was escorting Rosemary. He was beginning to walk. He carefully used his wobbly legs to trudge the distance. He was so cute.

"Yes we are," she said in between giggles. "He has been pulling up on everything in sight. It won't be long before he's on his own."

"Good, hopefully mine will be like that."

"Well honey, you gotta have one first." Yvonne looked at her watch. "Hurry and that way, you can quit your job to be at home with us." She was speaking of Susan, another housewife who lived down the street.

"I was looking to see what the date was. Give me about six more months."

"Until...what...you're not...ooh!" Rosemary squealed and let go of her own child to hug Yvonne. When they released, Jackson was sitting on the lawn, having fallen.

"Yes ma'am!"

"Victor is so excited, isn't he?"

"You already know he is." Yvonne was smiling so much, her face hurt.

"Honey, that's great. I know you are going to give up that job." Rosemary wanted Yvonne to join the ranks of the housewives clubs and socials that several women around Fayetteville were a part of.

"Slowly. My load will be decreased by half and I'm not taking any new homes after the next three months."

"Good, phase it out. Trust me, you'll want to spend as much time with the little one as you can. Any names yet?"

"Not a single one," Yvonne said silencing the ringer on her phone. There was still time left in the business day.

"Let me take this call Rosemary," Yvonne said hurriedly.

"Ok and don't forget, Susan and I take the boys out strolling four mornings a week," Rosemary added as a side note.

Yvonne knew that she had to tell Mary Louise about her pregnancy. She had absolutely no intent on working full time all the way through. Knowing that she had become one of Mary Louise's top producers, she earned the right to take a lengthy maternity leave.

"I have some good news to tell you." Yvonne said after she and Mary Louise finished going over some new ads for the home buyers book.

"What is that?"

"I am with child."

"You are?" Mary Louise asked pleasantly, she did a little dance in her plush swivel chair behind the desk. She knew that Yvonne and her husband were very much in love and wanted to start a family.

"Yes I am. I'm only 3 months, but I wanted to talk to you about maternity leave."

"Girl," Mary Louise shooed her, "take as much time as you like. You will always have a spot on my payroll. Don't you even worry."

"Thank you." Yvonne remembered eight years ago sitting in that very office spilling her guts to Mary Louise about her horrible childhood.

"I can't wait to see this child. He, she, it is going to be so loved. And spoiled, even if I have to do it myself." Mary Louise came from behind the desk and gave Yvonne a great big hug. She was so happy for Yvonne.

Victor had been trying to call Monique since Saturday. She was not answering, nor was she returning his calls. He figured that she was upset because he pulled out of the agreement of supposedly taking her to get the procedure done. Her feelings were the last thing on his mind. All he cared about was that the deed was done.

Monique did not have the heart to tell Victor that she had not gone through with it. She knew just how much her having that abortion meant to him. Really, it was his whole lively hood. There was no way that he would be able to keep the child a secret from his wife forever. Eventually, the truth would have to come out that Monique had been there all along.

She also knew that she could not avoid him eternally. He was going to have to know that she did not go through with it. Telling him face to face was not an option, so she decided on telling him the same way she told him that she was pregnant.

The phone call was not an easy one to make. The longer she put it off, the more upset he would be when he found out. She wanted to relish in his anger, but it was more about her than him. Monique could not bring herself to harm that child. The only way the procedure would have taken place was if he had actually taken her. Since he did not bother to show support, she figured he really did not care whether or not she had the abortion. He obviously was not too interested in protecting his future.

"Mr. Russell."

"Hello Ms. Crenshaw, you've been avoiding me." He was gleeful. He thought she was calling to give him the good news.

"With good reason."

"What reason is that?" He was playing dumb, but he did not care. As far as he knew, the problem had been gotten rid of. Any resulting emotional backlash he could deal with.

"You lied to me."

"I had every intention of taking you, something came up and I could not maneuver it in our favor."

"Our? You don't care about our favor."

"Are you feeling okay? Did everything go as planned?"

"No, I'm still pregnant." As soon as the words escaped her lips, his world stopped spinning. Again. He thought that his mind had reverted back to when he was sitting in his car and he heard the words come out of her mouth initially.

"I'm sorry, I think I heard you wrong. What did you say?" He switched the phone to the other ear. His well manicured hand began to mildly twitch.

"You heard me. I did not have an abortion."

"What the hell do you mean by that?" He jumped up and closed his office door.

"I am still pregnant with your child, Victor Russell." She spelled it out for him.

"Monique we agreed that it was best for us if you did not have that child."

"No, it was best for you. All you care about is saving your image and your marriage."

"At least I have something worth protecting."

"Now is not the time for your little snide remarks. I found out that I was more than three months along," the truth was stretched.

"So?"

"So, that meant I was actually killing the child. I could not go through with that." She could hear Victor mumbling under his breath on the other end of the line. She had butterflies in her stomach the entire time that they were on the phone and she knew that he had a fire going on in his soul right now.

Victor started scratching his head. He knew that he could have gotten out of being with Yvonne that morning. He just did not want to. Now he was kicking himself in the butt for not going. How could he have been so stupid? So careless? Now his future rested in this crazy, jealous woman's womb and she was blaming her unwillingness to go through with the abortion on being too far along. If Monique were standing in front of him, he would have choked her. She did the right thing to call.

"You're still pregnant?" He asked in a low voice.

"Yes."

"Monique, what do you want from me?" He was beginning to feel like the whole thing had been a set up.

"For you to take care of your child." He knew it. She wanted money. The same thing they all wanted. Money that he worked so hard for to take care of his wife and child.

"It's not too late to go have it done, you know."

"Oh, you think that you can put me on the back burner and then only deal with me when it's convenient for you? It doesn't work that way."

"Monique we need to get this taken care of."

"You should have thought about that on Saturday." Monique hung up the phone. She had nothing else to say to him. She knew that Victor was just going to try to convince her to have an abortion again. There was no way that she was going to let him back her into a corner like he did before.

Victor held the dead phone to his ear until the busy alert started ringing. Once he finally hung it up, he turned his chair around to the window. He felt like he wanted to jump. He thought about their whole relationship, from the beginning. He wondered how it ever got this far. He wondered what his future was like. He wondered how Yvonne was going to react to the news when she found out.

Chapter 5

Yvonne was beginning to notice that her husband was behaving oddly. She could have attributed it to his becoming a father and anticipating all that came along with it. Victor was having restless nights of sleep. All night long, he would toss and turn keeping both himself and his wife awake. When he did seemingly drift into a bout of snoozing, it did not last long and it was dotted with sweat.

Under his eyes told the tales of his lackluster nights. Not only physically, but he was tired emotionally as well. He was known around the office for his personality and smile. His quick witted humor made the ladies blush, however not as of late. The peppy step that he used to enter the office everyday had slowed down and his salutations were from repetition, not from the heart.

At home when they were trying to spend quality time or hang out, Yvonne observed that he appeared to be spaced out, like she was not in the room. She would have to repeat herself again and again, often calling his name to get attention. His symptoms were gradual, but once they all came together, it was clear that something was going on.

Of course, whenever she would inquire about what was troubling him, the answers would vary, but they were all nonsense. "I'm stressed out at work," or "I'm worried about the baby," even "I don't know what kind of father I will be." The latter was a more believable reason since he did not have a father or father figure in his life. Parenting was something that he really wanted to do but was unsure of what kind of skills he possessed and further, what skills he lacked.

Yvonne was concerned about him. Whatever was really eating away at him, he was not saying and she could find no evidence that there was truly any rationale behind any of it. She had known Victor for years and had never seen him like this. As a matter of fact, he was always the one calming her down.

Preparing for the wedding, Yvonne had lost her mind. She was two steps away from killing her wedding planner, who was a doozy, the florist who got her flower arrangements completely wrong, and the caterer who was so late that he barely had time to set up before the guests walked into the reception hall. The entire time, Victor was holding her hand, whispering sweet nothings in her ear to take her mind away from everything.

One day after work, Victor walked in, loosened his tie and grabbed a beer from the fridge before walking around the couch to join Yvonne who was just sitting there silently. He noticed the T.V. was off and there was only one light on, which was in her office by the front door casting a shadow into the living room. There were candles spread around the room, just five or six, but the scent was inescapable. He took a deep, cleansing breath. When he got to the couch, he noticed 'the rug' on the floor. 'The rug' was their passionate escape. Whoever put out the rug was telling the other that it was really going down.

"Baby, I'm not in the mood," Victor started.

"Lay down," his wife instructed.

"Baby."

"You haven't been in the mood. I'm not asking you, I'm telling you to lay your self down."

"Whatever," he mumbled and gently placed his beer on the end table. He assumed the position which was normally on his back.

"Turn over."

"Oh, we're going to be freaky, huh?" He was trying to make light of it. The next thing he knew, she was pouring something warm all over his back. He figured it was the candle wax.

"Not exactly," she replied laughing. "Not freaky, relaxing."

"Hmm," he moaned. She rubbed the oil all over his back, then proceeded to sensually knead it. It had been a while since Yvonne had given her husband a massage. His shoulders and neck were quite tense. Whatever was wrong with him, she was now convinced that it was not in his mind. Using alternating rhythms, she continued to instrumentally take it all away. Her fingertips traveled up and down his spine and at last stroked his neck. The oil just made her hands move with more ease.

Even though there was not much light, she would still see the contrast of her hands on his caramel colored skin. She moved all around the neatly tapered hair line at the nape of her husband's neck.

Victor actually appreciated the fact that his wife was trying make him feel better. He was trying to relax and calm himself down as she was oiling him back up. His mind was polluted with the adulterous web that he had tangled around him. Not just another woman, but another baby too.

He wanted so bad to tell Yvonne, it was the only thing that he kept from her. When he did build up almost enough courage to tell her, he looked at her and saw the love in her eyes which just shut him down. Telling her now would definitely soften the blow. Victor could not let the words escape from his lips.

Yvonne made the session last as long as she could before kissing him on the forehead and pushing herself off of the floor. Her belly was discernable at five months and still had quite a ways to go. She was careful to use the edge of the couch to assist her up.

"Thank you Baby, I needed that."

"You're welcome. Go drink a couple cups of water to wash out the toxins and then take a shower. If you lay down, you may be able to actually sleep tonight."

"What about dinner?"

"Are you hungry?"

"Just a little."

"After you shower, I'll have something ready." Victor did as he was instructed and when he got out of the shower she had prepared him a chicken salad. She wanted to fix him something light so he could sleep well.

Yvonne tried to stay out of Victor's way for the next couple of days. She wanted him to know that he had privacy, praying the space would prompt him to just be open and honest with her. Everyday that he walked out of the door, she hoped that when he came back, he would be the same man that she married.

His relationship with Monique was very much the same. He had not touched her since before she announced that she was pregnant. Besides the fact that he made her bring him an ultrasound from her obstetrician, he did not want to have anything to do with her. At first, he thought that she wanted to claim to be pregnant just to get attention away from his expecting wife. The ultrasound, delivered to him in person, proved otherwise. It was not just a claim, she really was pregnant.

Every time his caller ID said 'Crenshaw', he cringed. It made him sick to his stomach. He used to look forward to her calls and impromptu lunch dates. Now, his attitude towards her was disgust. Not so much with her, but more with himself for letting it get to that point. In three years, he had not been careless, he thought. The truth was, he had been careless for some time, it was only just catching up with him.

Monique was not totally surprised that he treated her like a leper. It was, after all, her final decision not to have an abortion. He called to check on her. Their conversations were short lived and she could tell that they were not from the heart. He felt that he had to keep up a certain façade. She was a woman who had his life, as he knew it, in her hands. She knew where he worked and she knew how they felt about family at Bowles and Laughton. She knew where he lived. She knew about his wife, where her office was and that she primarily worked out of the home. Even if Yvonne wanted to deny all of that, she could not deny the DNA that Monique carried inside of her.

Keeping up a happy face at work had become nearly impossible and at home even more so. The only time he could be himself was at Sparky's. He would walk in the door and straight to the bar. Sonya felt bad for him, but it was a predicament that was totally avoidable. She fixed him the usual and he would go and play a round of pool by himself. In every facet of his life, he was not talking much. Guilt was eating him alive.

In the week since Yvonne had given him a massage, he had come home on three occasions and spread out the rug himself. She smiled at him sprawled out like a crucifix just waiting on her. It made her believe that he was beginning to come around. She wanted to help him snap out of whatever it was because she was going to need him to be on top of his game. And soon. She called him at work shortly after lunchtime and told him that Sparky's was out tonight and he needed to come straight home.

His first thought was that Monique had finally gotten to her. Her tone, in the phone call was not urgent or upset. Not having the energy to question or disobey, he left work early. He chose to go ahead and get it over with. Upon his arrival, he was surprised to find a suitcase sitting by the door and Yvonne's purse and keys on the stand in the hallway.

"Yvonne!" He called out in bewilderment. He then turned directly into her home office.

"Yes," she responded gathering some papers off of the printer.

"What the hell is going on! What is that suitcase doing sitting by the door? Where are you going?" His eyes were wild. The papers, the suitcase, he thought she was leaving. She could see that she sparked confusion. At least she knew that he still had emotions.

"No, that's for you."

"For me? What the hell for? I didn't do anything!"

"You're right. Lately, you haven't done anything. Look at you, you don't talk to me anymore, you don't spend time with me anymore. Victor, you haven't even touched me in going on two months. You don't sleep, you hardly eat. After work you go hang out and I don't see you until after the street lights are on. I feel like I live alone."

"So what, you're kicking me out?" His face revealed his trepidation.

"No Baby," she then smiled to let him know everything was alright. "I'm taking you somewhere. I couldn't lift the suitcase. Well, I didn't want to. Use the bathroom, we have a long drive ahead of us.

By the time they got situated and the car loaded, it was a little bit after 3. The drive was going to take right at 4 and a half hours. She put in a relaxing neo soul CD and hit the highway. Victor asked her where was she taking him, she told him that he would see soon enough. He was completely puzzled with a suitcase, an oversized beach bag with a knotted dark garbage bag inside concealing its contents and a cooler. Whatever it was, she had taken her time to plan.

Two bathroom stops and 3 CD's later, they pulled off of the interstate. The last sign that Victor had seen said 'Welcome to Tennessee', so he knew that they had crossed state lines. When they were exiting, they hit a huge bump in the road which awakened him. They rode down a two lane highway for a few miles and then turned onto a dirt road. The only scenery was acres and acres of lush green timber. The road led them out to a clearing in the woods. She stopped at the first log cabin that she saw. Yvonne told him not to get out, she would handle everything.

Victor had a look on his face that said a thousand adjectives of sheer perplexity. He thought about all the programs Yvonne had him watch where he had seen several times on T.V. that the husband or wife took their spouse out for a nice vacation and then killed them. He had to chuckle at the thought of Yvonne killing him. *What would she have to gain? Nothing, well, there is the $500,000 life insurance policies,* he thought. *We did just increase them after finding out that she was pregnant.*

He shot the idea out of his head when he saw her walking hurriedly to the car with a grin as wide as the Nile is long. There were several cabins scattered on the property. They were close enough to see, yet each had trees around to offer a bit of privacy. Yvonne drove him down the driveway past those to a more secluded area. The cabins were getting more and more spread out with the dense forest between them also increasing. Finally, when it looked like they were nearing the end of the driveway, she turned onto another driveway labeled with an arrow made of wood and bright yellow paint.

Driving slowly on the road, she made the first right turn that she came to. As she paid close attention to what she was doing, Victor was curious as to where the road they were just on trailed off to. When he bought his interest back to what was before them, he saw a single cabin that had a small circumference of clearing around it.

"Ready?" Yvonne said, tapping her acrylic nails on her wood steering wheel.

"I guess."

"You guess?" her voice was very animated. "You are going to enjoy yourself! C'mon, take your stuff out of the trunk." He got his belongings and followed her into the cabin.

"Victor," she began, "this is your crib for the next three nights. There is a breathtaking view of the mountains reflecting off the lake behind here." She proceeded to the back of the cabin and opened the blinds.

"Damn." He was impressed with what he saw.

"You also have a Jacuzzi on the porch and a pool table in the play room. There are rocking chairs inside and out. A nice leather couch to parlay on," she pointed back to the living room as they made their way through the house. "A fully stocked kitchen."

"So that's what is in the cooler," he said.

"The beach bag has your dry food. The picnic basket has fresh fruits and salad, the cooler has precooked meals that I slaved over since you left for work this morning. There is enough food for about a week, in case you get lunchy."

"Baby..."

"I also have here," she shoved a bookbag at him, "about twenty DVD's for you to watch. So you don't have to leave the cabin if you don't want to. You have everything here except a computer which would defeat the purpose of you being here." He stood there and took in his surroundings. It was nice and spacious. Yvonne had even gone the extra mile to make sure that he had seclusion and no mental distractions.

"Wow," he was sincerely speechless.

"Oh and there is a land line for you to call up to the main cabin. They have a sort of taxi service if you *need* anything. They will take you up the street to the store or to the National State Park not far from here. Here are two of the brochures for that, if you want to get out and stretch your legs." She laid them on the table and looked up towards the ceiling trying to see if she was forgetting to tell him anything.

"Where will you be?"

"Home, I have to call you in sick from work tomorrow."

"You can do that from here, with me." He walked over to her and grabbed her hand. She was seeing a change already.

"No, I can't. This reservation is for one."

"They don't have to know you're staying."

"They don't care, I do. I think you need your battery recharged. This should do the trick. You have nothing to keep you from relaxation except you. Turn your phone off and call me just to keep in touch. Today is Thursday, I'll be back to pick you up Sunday at 4." Her smile was so sweet.

"Yvonne, don't leave me way out here. I don't even know where I am," he said looking worried.

"Townsend, Tennessee. Believe me, you are safer out here than you are at home. The other people out here are trying to get away just like you. The doors have a million locks on them and the windows are all covered. I love you." She pecked him on the lips and dismissed herself.

Victor watched her Lexus kick up dirt as she backed out and left. He felt so empty and alone. *Yvonne was probably right*, he thought, *this is just what I need.* He took the food out of the carriers that it was in and put it up. The next order or business was to take a shower and really begin his vacation. He settled on trying to make the best of it because whether or not he liked it, he was stuck out there.

Yvonne had packed him several pair of sweats and lounging clothes and only one outfit. If he wanted to go out, he had to make it worth his while. He threw on a pair of sweats and popped in a movie. She had a couple goodies like popcorn and sour candy for the movies that she packed for him. He took full advantage.

Not neglecting his expectant wife, he called her every thirty minutes to make sure that she was okay on the road. He noticed when choosing a picture that she had a nice range. There were inspirational movies, a few action thrillers and a majority were light hearted 'chick flicks' and comedies.

When she at last made it home, he knew that he could rest peacefully. He could not wrap his mind around what she had done. His wife had conceived to plan him the ultimate getaway without her. She even cooked him food for the entire stay. What astonished him the most was that she did the entire thing without mentioning one word to him.

Victor knew that he had to get his act together, sooner than later. This was an extreme measure. There was no explanation behind his wife having to plan him an escape 200 miles away all by his lonesome. It just did not make any sense. Was he acting that aloof? Had his demeanor changed that drastically? Yvonne was basically crying out to him. Her cry was extremely loud.

He certainly planned to take advantage of her effort. The entire time he was there, away from the city, away from familiar surroundings, it hit him just how bad off he seemed. That, in turn, made him more determined to make a change.

He awakened Friday morning feeling more rested. He slept at least half of the night, which was an adjustment from the previous two months. The sun rays were warm on his body, shaving off the morning chill leftover from the night. Victor was in no rush to jump out of bed. There were no briefs to be filed, no phone calls to return, just nature.

Before he could make peace with anybody else, he had to make peace with himself. He tried to persuade Monique to get rid of the baby. She did not and now was too late. Yes, he had an affair, but staying away from Monique was just going to make her even more angry. Yvonne certainly did not deserve to get the short end of the stick. She loved him and was an awesome wife to him.

He was left with a choice to make and three days to get it together. He rolled out of bed and grabbed an apple for breakfast, then plopped on the couch to watch another movie. For the next three days, he lounged and relaxed. He did not have to worry about anything, being totally removed from the outside world. He soaked in the Jacuzzi both Friday and Saturday nights. There was a nature trail that he enjoyed twice a day on all three days. He saw deer and other wildlife out there in the woods.

The pool table did not lack attention. He played a game in between each movie to keep him from becoming a complete couch potato. The most intimate time that he experienced was on the back porch. He sat in the wooden rocker and looked at the vast mountains before him. The calm lake separating him from the mountains. The trees that swayed in the breeze. He made peace with himself and his decisions. He would just have to go forward and play with the cards that he was dealt.

When Yvonne arrived to pick him up, they were both very happy to see each other. Victor was sitting on the front porch waiting on his wife to swing in any minute. He looked like a whole new man. She knew right then that she had made the right choice to take him to Townsend. She certainly had missed him. The house was lonely just knowing that she would not see him at night, even if their communication had been slighted. Her husband meant the world to her and if she could cut off a depression, she would.

He waltzed down the steps to meet her. He scooped her up and walked her inside the house, straight to the bedroom. She was yelling at him to put her down the whole time. He ignored her and finally laid her across the bed.

"Okay?" She said. He hovered over her and looked into her eyes. The woman that he vowed to love, the woman he betrayed.

"Thank you."

"You're welcome," she said giggling.

"I really, really needed this."

"I know. That's why I did it."

"I feel like a new man," he said earnestly. Feeling absolutely revived.

"Good. Now let me up, you're driving back."

"Don't you want to enjoy some of nature with me."

"I already did, vicariously."

"That's not what I mean." He leaned in and began to kiss her passionately. She was caught off guard. That did not stop her from reciprocating. The kisses were full and had true emotion behind them. She rubbed her hands up and down his back as her head angled to have complete access of his lips. He ended with a couple pecks and encouraged her to go out with him and just see the type of atmosphere that had been at his disposal.

She obliged him and hand in hand, they started out. Unknowingly, she was dressed perfectly for the occasion. She had on a sports skirt and short sleeve jacket with a tank top underneath. Her well toned legs extended into her tennis shoes. Her outfit was yellow, which was a compliment to her light skin and a yellow ponytail holder. The curls of her hair tumbled down her back.

Victor walked her around on a course in the forest. They were talking about what had been going on in their lives since they had last seen each other. Victor apologized sincerely for the way that he had been acting. Of course, his wife forgave him. She, in turn, described how their baby had been kicking her. He took her to a rising where she could get a good view of the lake and all the trees that enveloped them. It was simply magnificent. She took in a deep breath of the great outdoors.

He took her into his arms and began kissing her again. He held her face in both of his hands and explored her mouth with deep intent. He took one of his hands and unzipped the outer shell of the skirt suit just a bit. He stuck his hand under her tank top and on her naked breast. Her breathing got heavier. He massaged her and kissed her deeper hoping to convey how much he needed her.

She could feel that he was maturing and put her hand inside his pants. He was pulsating in her hand. She was being stirred from the pit of her soul. He turned her away from him. From behind, Victor licked down her ears until his juicy lips met with her neck. There was a mild breeze that blew past them. The rustle of the leaves, quieted her moans and the wind stimulated her already hardened nipples.

They were both yearning and panting, grinding on each other. He reached for her panties and pulled them down. Yvonne grabbed hold of the tree beside her and positioned himself in a stance, feet shoulder width apart. Victor slid inside of her, gently because he met a bit of resistance since he had not touched her in so long. Once he was all the way contained by her luscious walls, he let out a loud groan. All he could think about was how long it had been for him, for the both of them. He stroked and stroked and she held her stance, leaning into the tree.

She arrived. He knew the sounds of her climax all too well. Yvonne then found a stump on the ground and propped her foot on it. Having more access to her, he began to have his way with her. One of his hands was delicately placed around her neck and the other on her hip. She began to shudder again, but refused to let out a sound. The excitement of being out in the wild was doing wonders for them. Knowing they could be spotted at any time just heightened their sensitivity. Yvonne had never done anything like that.

"Its run...running...running down my leg," she whimpered about her love fluids. He could hear the sound her body made every time he thrust and pulled away.

"You're so wet," he whispered back to her, further acknowledging what they both by now knew.

"Cum with me, baby, cum with me." By coaxing him, she knew that it would drive him over the edge. She was certainly there, having peaked twice already. She took her free hand and rubbed up and down his leg. Victor contorted his neck to kiss her. No sooner than he did, he could feel himself explode from deep within his loins. She, at the same time, experienced a profound pleasure that made her finally scream out.

After collecting themselves, they walked hand and hand back to the cabin where Victor loaded the car and drove them back to their home in Fayetteville, Georgia.

Monique had been waiting on Victor to come by. He called her the day before and told her he wanted to see her, after first calming her down, because his cell phone had been off for several days.

"If you're worried about me suing you for child support, you don't have to worry about that," was the first thing out of her mouth when she opened the door.

"Who said anything about that?"

"You have been avoiding me for the longest."

"I told you, Yvonne..."

"Oh yeah, Yvonne took you on some damn romantic getaway in the woods somewhere."

"No, she left me in a cabin in Tennessee by myself, to get my head together. She was concerned about me."

"She wasn't too concerned, or she would have been meeting all of your needs in the first place."

"Look Nique, I did not come here to let you brow beat my innocent wife," Victor said sternly.

"I'm innocent too," he laughed at her. "I was concerned about you. I just don't have access to you like she does."

"I know," he said settling on the couch. He pulled Monique in his arms over to him and kissed her on the head. He was trying to smooth things over, he knew that she had a vindictive side.

"I really just had to get my head together. Having two babies and my wife only knows about one is a lot of pressure on a man."

"I can't imagine. I don't, ahem, we don't need much from you."

"Don't worry about it, Big Vic is gonna take care of you."

"Ooh, please do," she said in a sensual voice. Being pregnant, she was still looking good and from the back, he could not even tell that she was pregnant. She answered the door in a pair of tangerine colored boy shorts and ribbed tank top with no bra on underneath. Monique's well endowed breasts pressed against the thin white undershirt.

"Did you cook?"

"We can eat later," she started unbuttoning his shirt.

"I'm hungry now." He pushed her back and she looked at him strangely.

"You know, just because I said that I was not going to put you on child support does not mean that I still won't take your life away from you."

"Take my life away?" He asked like he was sure that she was just calling his bluff. "Don't get it twisted

Nique, I know that you might have the upper hand right now, but I don't take threats lightly. All I did was ask you for something to eat and there you go jumping off on a tangent."

"Where have you been for the last month? Am I supposed to go through this pregnancy by myself? Typical niggas, man," she mumbled angrily under her breath.

"I have been M.I.A. from every aspect of my life recently. Do you understand what kind of pressure I'm under?" He began to raise his voice, "You chose to go through with this pregnancy, so forgive me if I spend most of my free time with my wife! You are only going through with this by yourself because you wanted to go through with it. You had my total support to end this, you made the decision on your own to keep this child!"

"This child? It's your child, too!"

"But I did not want it! Somehow you keep forgetting that!" Now they were both standing up in a confrontational mode.

"Victor I don't know why I even put up with you. You are a piece of trash! You are a sad excuse for a man!" Monique said shaking her head to herself.

"Leave me!" He said with his arms outstretched. "I never asked you to stay! At any point during this whole relationship, you could have just walked away. As a matter of fact, the last time I remember the relationship being in question, you were the one who came crawling back to me." His remarks were smug. What he said was stinging her to the core, but he was right. Her mind flashed back to the times that she went back to him apologetically.

"Get out my house!"

"What was that?" He put his hand behind his ear mimicking that he could not hear her.

"Get out of my house! Don't come back!" Those words were music to Victor's ears. He got up and was out of the door quicker than lightening.

On the way back home, he knew that she would not abort the baby being more than halfway through the gestation. All he was doing by walking away was making his unborn child another statistic. He had to go back and undo what he had just done. If he did not, Monique was going to have her claws so deep in his skin that he would not know what hit him. Fifteen minutes after the blow out, he was knocking on the door. Monique opened the door with a tear stained face.

"Look, I know that we both hate this situation that we are in, but I guess we have to make the best of it. I don't want things to go down like this." Victor spoke from the other side of the threshold, he was not invited in.

"They don't have to," she said weakly.

"That's my child and I guess I have to do what's right by this child."

"It's a boy."

"A boy?" He asked surprised, pushing passed her to get inside.

"Yep."

"I will do what I can for him. I think you and I need to call it quits." Monique put her face in her hands and started crying again. The only reason he turned around was simply to keep the peace. He was not afraid of Monique, but he feared what she was capable of.

"Why?"

"You know this is something that we should have done a long time ago. We need to do this thing with clear heads. We can't do that with passion clouding our judgment."

"Whatever, Victor."

"I want to be cool, friends even." He sat down beside her and tried to comfort her. Monique did not want his reassurance.

"Just leave," she pleaded again.

"I'm not leaving until you tell me that we can be cool." He was really playing her.

"Leave."

"Nope."

"Ok...ok...cool."

"Alright," he gave her a kiss on the forehead and left. This time a lot more peacefully.

As usual, Alicia was Monique's shoulder. They joined each other for lunch and in between bites, Monique gave her blow for blow of the argument between she and Victor. Alicia listened to the entire thing, nodding her head and giving the occasional 'umm hmm.' It was therapeutic for Monique to have someone she could count on.

Alicia combated Monique's tale with her own soap opera. She gave accounts of her photographed subjects and the wedding bloopers that she witnessed first hand. Monique would have been quickly bored if she did not need the comic relief. Monique quickly reverted the attention back to her.

"I need to find out what OB she goes to."

"For what?" Alicia was completely puzzled.

"Maybe I could bump into her." Monique said with inclusive optimism.

"And what good would that do?"

"You don't think that she has a right to know that her husband is having an affair with me?"

"Let you tell it, its *had* an affair and it's over."

"The affair is over, but the effects sure aren't."

"You just get so much joy in that poor woman's ignorance. She's just like most of the married women in America whose husbands cheat. She has no idea."

"I think she needs to."

"I don't think that you are the one who should tell her."

"Why not?" Monique asked defensively.

"Put yourself in her shoes," Alicia began. "She doesn't know you from Adam and she meets you at the OB's office. Why would she believe that you are carrying her husband's child?"

"Son," Monique corrected.

"Son. I mean, if I were her, I would think that you are a crazy groupie or something."

"Yeah, but when I send her the paternity test..." Monique looked at her friend knowing that was the undeniable evidence.

"Then he'll apologize like his life depends on it, because it does and she will forgive him. Don't you remember how you apologized and he took you back. It's the same scenario. Trust me when I tell you, he will do whatever it takes to get her back."

"I'm sure it won't work."

"And if it doesn't, then you won't be on his list of things to do. Once you are nabbed as the culprit for the breakup, he will not want to have anything to do with you." Alicia took a sip of her sweet tea to let it soak through her friend's thick skull.

"I guess you're right," Monique had to drag from deep within.

"You know I'm right. C'mon girl, you are better than that. If she finds out, she finds out. Whatever elaborate plot you have to get the guy won't work. Only he can decide to leave her for you and honestly if he hasn't yet, it probably won't happen." The declaration was a hard pill to swallow, but it made perfect sense.

Now late in the seventh month, Yvonne was certainly beginning to feel the effects of carrying a human being inside of her. Her stomach was unmistakably distended and her bathroom breaks were frequent. She had a glow about her that Victor thought was absolutely fantastic. She had four more homes on her roster, then she would be taking her maternity leave. Mary Louise Parker was letting Yvonne do things in her own time.

The Russells had no idea what they were going to name her either. The fetus had not cooperated with the ultrasound and they were oblivious to her sex until a week ago. Armed with that knowledge, Yvonne began jotting down first and middle names that she liked. She was sitting down to the list when she heard him pull up.

Victor came home with a bag full of clothes which he threw in the corner. He ran upstairs. Yvonne, curious to see what goodies her husband got his hands on this time went over to the bag. It was filled with onesies and newborn clothes that were blue and green. That would have been nice, but they were having a girl.

"Baby, what happened to pinks and yellows?" Yvonne was trying to figure out why he bought the colors he did.

"Oh, those are not for our baby."

"Ok," Yvonne was taken aback.

"There is a paralegal at the firm who is pregnant. Her baby's daddy is a dead beat, so you know me." He responded implementing himself as a goodwill Samaritan.

"Yeah, always trying to save the world." She put the clothes back into the bag and went over to him.

"Why am I married to such a good man?" She asked rubbing her hands on his smooth caramel skin.

"I guess you just got lucky, huh?" He took one of her hands and kissed inside the palm.

"I guess. What about Simone Alexandria?"

"For what, the new epic heroine blockbuster this summer?"

"No silly, our daughter."

"No."

"How about Anna Marie?"

"We are not Spanish."

"Ok, LaShavanitria?"

"Ooh, say it again more slowly." Victor exclaimed with his face lit up.

"La-Sha-va-nee-tree-a." He knew she was trying to be funny.

"Hell to the naw! I need my daughter to be able to get a job. Even further, she needs to be able to spell her name before age 10," they both laughed.

"Jordan?"

"No soul."

"Zana?"

"Too foreign."

"X?"

"While you're playing, you might be for real. It will be easy for her to write her signature."

"Kalia?"

"Kalia what?"

"I haven't gotten that far yet."

"I like that," Victor approved.

"Yeah," Yvonne wiggled her pregnant belly all around. They had finally settled on a name.

Wondering why her husband was buying clothes for a pregnant para at the job that she had never heard of, curiosity got the best of Mrs. Victor Russell. She decided to probe deeper into the situation. Yvonne knew, just as well as everyone else did that Ms. Betsy knew everything that was happening on her floor and most of the others. She had such a sweet motherly way about her, everybody trusted her and rarely was her name ever attached to spread rumors.

"Good morning Ms. Betsy. Its Yvonne."

"Hello, Dear. Victor told me that you bought him that new sunshine yellow shirt and paisley tie that he's wearing today," Ms. Betsy knew exactly who as on the phone. Yvonne had always been kind to her and Ms. Betsy knew they could joke around.

"Yes ma'am," both ladies were laughing. Yvonne could tell where the conversation was headed.

"I told him it takes a real man to wear that," Ms. Betsy burst into a fit of laughter.

"It's Burberry, the tie was on sale. I bought him another one almost just like it. Trust me, you'll know it when you see it."

"Oh dear," Ms. Betsy was catching her breath, "I can't wait!"

"Last night, Victor said something about a pregnant para up there."

"Pregnant para? No ma'am, you must have misunderstood. Surprisingly, there's not a pregnant woman in the building."

"Oh, he must have meant a pregnant client, you know his mind isn't good."

"I told him to take Echinacea for that," the elder lady chuckled.

"Could you transfer me to my husband, please?"

"Sure thing." As Ms. Betsy transferred the call, Yvonne hung up. Her husband had lied to her. She knew that she heard him correctly when he said that he was buying the baby clothes for a pregnant paralegal at his office.

The news hit her hard. She sat there and pondered why her husband would lie to her. She certainly did not know anybody who was expecting a boy, other than the women in her Lamaze class. He would not be buying them anything. Then she began to think back to when he was going through his severe withdrawal. Could this woman have anything to do with all that? Of course not, she dismissed the whole idea out of her head.

Chapter 6

Giving birth to this child was without a doubt going to be the highlight of Yvonne's life. All of her attention was devoted to making every detail about the birth perfect. Everyday, she rubbed her belly and talked to her daughter. Yvonne encouraged her to give her mother an easy labor. The emergency bag was packed in her trunk, she had gone to Lamaze classes and spoken to other moms about their experiences. Susan and Rosemary did not have any horror stories to add.

The house was a whole different story. Yvonne hired a cleaning service to come give her house the once over total cleaning, even after she had already removed just about every germ and dust bunny. One of the spare bedrooms was converted to a nursery. She was well aware that for the first few months, Kalia would be sleeping in the bed with her or in the bassinette beside her. That did not stop her from going all out preparing a room for her pampered princess.

Victor did not stop her either. What she wanted to do was all up to her. He loved the fact that she was so excited and he tried to share in the joy with her. He did quite a good job disguising his true feelings. He was excited about his daughter while trying to hide the hurt about his son. He, too, would rub Yvonne's oversized belly and talk to his daughter. Earlier in the pregnancy Kalia would kick in response to the attention. Now though, she was in the delivery position. There was not enough room to get rowdy. Yvonne could not wait to see her.

Neither could Victor's co-workers. The event happy Senior Bowles approved Ms. Betsy's notion to have a baby shower for the couple. This shin ding took place after work at a restaurant and was very well attended. The Russells got every possible thing that they needed. After the baby shower, there was nothing left to buy.

In the eighth month, Yvonne completely cut her activities down to almost zilch. Her stomach was so protruded that now she had the pregnant woman's waddle. She had to scoot to the edge of her seats to get up whether she had Victor to aid her or not. Getting in and out of the car was an episode in itself. Although she was enthused to be carrying a child, she would be exhilarated once Kalia finally came.

On the other side of town, Monique was arranging her life to be a single mother. Emotionally, the two women were in two different worlds. She had been thinking a lot about how expensive things were going to be more so than enjoying the experience. She was second guessing the decision that she made to keep her son. Her job paid the bills, but providing for an infant was very costly. How was she going to provide for him alone? What if Victor was not around like he promised? Why was Yvonne still holding on so tightly?

She had a small baby shower with a few friends and co-workers, nothing near the scale that Victor got from Bowles and Laughton. Victor, so far, kept good on his word and had been buying the baby things. She managed to add to the necessities on her slightly more than meager salary. Still, this was not what she had envisioned for her life when she thought about family and future.

Monique was so jealous of Yvonne getting to live the high life with the fine man in the big house driving a luxury car. Monique knew that she could get all of that if she just opened herself up a little. She had all of her bread in one oven and that oven was not on. She could not blame her predicament on anyone else. She had more than ample time to get herself out of the situation. At times, it seemed that Victor was inviting her to go find a life for herself.

Instead, she continued to cling to the false hopes of an ideal world that she evolved herself. Now the atmosphere around her involved more than just her, there was an innocent bystander as well. Every single decision that she made from here on out would have some effect on her son. She knew that she had to pull herself together to be the strong mother that her child would need. Her motivation was the very second beat within her.

"It won't be much longer," Alicia said to her friend.
"I know, I can't wait!"
"You look like you are about to drop any minute." Alicia egged her on while patting her rigid abdomen.
"I feel like I am. Look at my ankles, girl." Monique pointed down.
"Ooh, I do not envy you. I wonder if you are going to loose all your baby weight right away."
"I hope so. Listen, let me ask you a question."
"Ok, shoot."
"How would you feel about having an adorable, sweet, innocent roommate?"
"Do you want to get me a dog?"
"No, Alicia. I don't think I should stay in this apartment with this baby by myself. I just wouldn't feel very safe."

"Are you trying to set me up to be your in-house babysitter? Cause if you are, I do work and my schedule is unpredictable."

"You make your own schedule, so I'm not worried about that. Financially, I just think that it would be better for both of us if we stayed together. You do get jobs, but they aren't steady. This way both of us could save money and get better on our feet." Monique was pleading her case. She had been thinking about this for a long time.

"Hmm, a roommate. I'm still confused as to who the adorable, innocent roommate would be. You are crazy and your child will be annoying."

"Alicia that is so wrong."

"What, you don't think so? All that crying and carrying on. Please. When do you want to move in?"

"We can wait til after I heal from the birth. I'm too big to worry about packing and lifting anything."

"I think you just might have a deal. I don't mind the baby. My room will be at the other end of the house."

"Great! You better not renege on me."

"You mean like Victor? Speaking of, what are you going to name your son?" Alicia wanted to throw a blow in there, then quickly move on.

"I do not know. I've come up with a couple names, but I'm not completely sold on any of them." In her heart of hearts, Monique really wanted to name her son after Victor. She felt that it would be only fitting that his first son be named after him. She also surmised that it would give her an edge should she have to go through the drastic effort of getting child support. Regardless of her word to Victor that she would not sue him for support, she was not above it. His household could certainly stand to loose a little income. Yvonne would not even miss it, Monique was sure.

Any name short of Victor just did not tug at her the same way. Victor Russell II. Monique recognized that it would be a stretch for a married man to name his illegitimate son after him. She wondered if there was any way that she could do it without him knowing. Victor would not sign the birth certificate without a name on it. The time would be upon them soon enough when they would have to make a choice.

"Guess who I ran into?" Richard Worthy saw Victor facing the urinal in the men's restroom. Victor looked around to see who Worthy could be talking to. He was sure that Worthy was not talking to him. Their relationship had never been the same since the incident with Monique at the job. It took Victor what seemed like a million years to be able to overcome the guilty feeling he got when he saw Senior Bowles. He felt like he had the scarlet letter written on his face.

"Aww, I wish you wouldn't be such a sore sport. Anyway, I bumped into Monique at the mall yesterday. Isn't that cool?" Worthy was still for all intents and purposes talking to himself. When Victor flushed the urinal, he went over to wash his hands. It was too early in the morning for this.

"She was pregnant. Very pregnant. I almost did not even recognize her." Worthy found himself heading over to the sink behind him. "She told me that she was doing very well and she and the baby's daddy were an item." He added a little extra oomph with 'baby's daddy.' Victor dried his hands off and walked out of the bathroom.

He knew exactly why Worthy brought Monique up. It was obvious that he saw her or he would not have known that she was expecting. Victor then had the answer that he had been looking for so long. It was Worthy who ratted him out to management before. Between Worthy trying to get an edge up and Monique being upset about the engagement to Yvonne, Victor was unsure how and why his secret was unearthed.

All Worthy wanted was a rise out of Victor. Their relationship was strictly professional and only when it was absolutely necessary. The entire firm knew that for whatever reason, Worthy and Victor did not work well together. So rarely did they have to. Victor skated back to his office and no sooner than he sat down and wheeled himself to the computer, Ms. Betsy came running to the door.

"Victor, it's Yvonne. She's at Crawford Long," she said with urgency.

"Crawford Long? But our hospital is..." He was trying to make sense of it all. He did not know what his wife was doing downtown.

"Never mind, Victor. You've got to go! That girl's gonna have a baby!" Victor's eyes widened and he gasped for air, like he was snapped into shock. It took him a second to realize what was going on. He jumped up and grabbed his suit jacket.

"Lock me up," he said hurriedly to Ms. Betsy on his way past her. She had a spare key to his office.

"Call me!" She yelled behind him down the hall. Ms. Betsy had a grin on her face thinking about the first time that she gave birth. The first child was so exciting, so new.

Victor ran down the hallway and pressed the button for the elevator. Then he pressed the button again. Then yet again. Finally, being impatient, he bolted through the emergency exit and shot down the stairs. He was in his car and on the street in the blink of an eye.

"Baby, Baby, what's going on?" Victor managed to call his wife.

"I was having lunch and..."

"Lunch with who?"

"By myself."

"Having lunch, where? You are due to drop a baby any day now! What are you doing having lunch by yourself?"

"I just had a craving, Victor. Plus, I just wanted to get out and move around. After the baby, I won't be able to go to Gladys Knight's for a good little while. I was trying to get some soul food while the getting was good."

"You were at a Gladys Knight's?" Victor asked in disbelief.

"Yeah, and my water broke. At least I finished my plate," she said trying to give herself something humorous to think about.

"How do you feel?"

"I'm cramping right now with every contraction, but it's getting worse." He could hear the discomfort in her voice. She was trying to hold it in and be strong, but it was already getting the best of her.

"Baby hold on, I'll be right there!" Victor closed up his phone and stepped on the gas. He looked at the time and realized that his wife must have gotten there as soon as the restaurant opened up for lunch. Usually by this time, he would still have a little ways to go before lunch.

He shook all that out of his head. He was not thinking about anything but getting to Yvonne's side swiftly and carefully. He could not get there fast enough. Every second that passed by seemed like an hour. By the time he got to the hospital, his heart was pounding out of his chest and his forehead was covered in sweat.

In what seemed like hours, he found his wife in labor. Kalia was coming. She was not waiting on anybody's permission. Victor had gone to Lamaze classes with Yvonne and was a good coach. She greatly appreciated his encouragement and just the comfort of him being there. She could not imagine how any woman could have a baby alone.

Both new parents-to-be had their minds totally focused on the task at hand. They were just as eager to see their bundle of joy as she was to stretch out her legs and explore the world. Victor could feel his cell phone vibrating on his hip. He was too concerned with what was going on to answer the calls. He figured that it was Ms. Betsy wondering how things were going so she could report back to the firm.

Soon, the vibration began to distract him from his coaching and he decided to power it off. Making Yvonne the center of his attention gave her the support that she needed to push. He had seen the videos, but he still was not prepared for what he witnessed. Bringing a person into the world was truly a miraculous happening.

There she was rolling around in the bed from side to side, groaning about her pain, with a pillow between her legs. That was the part that seemed to be routine. When Yvonne was moved to the delivery position with her legs propped up and she started squeezing Victor's hand for dear life. That is when he began to get nervous.

The contractions were running full throttle. He did not know what to expect, neither did she and when he realized that neither one of them had all their ducks in a row, he commenced to panic. The yelling and sweating and pushing threw him into a frenzy, but he was trying to keep it together for his young family.

The crowning was an event in itself. With every push Kalia was coming, however, Yvonne was having a hard time getting the head completely out. The nurses found a mirror and set it so that The Russells could see what was going on. It also gave Yvonne an intimate look at what was going on, persuading her to hold her push for just an extra second. The reflection paid off and Kalia Russell was escorted into the world with the help of her loving parents.

Yvonne was absolutely exhausted. The labor had gone late in the day, lasting just at 10 hours. Shortly after laying eyes on her princess in the flesh, Yvonne tapered off to sleep. Victor was worn out himself and went down to the cafeteria for something to eat. He remembered that his phone had been ringing off the hook earlier and turned it on so that he could listen to his voicemail. Ms. Betsy had left two messages of concern. He made a mental note to call her first thing in the morning.

"Victor...it's me...uh, uh, ooh...I'm at Crawford L...Long...call me!" It was Monique. Hearing the message, sent a pang to the pit of Victor's stomach. He thought, *how can this be happening*? What were the chances of both his children were being born at the same time in the same hospital?

He pressed the button to return the call to Monique. As the phone rang in his ear, he felt nauseous. Monique answered and said that she was okay and that his son was waiting to see him.

Instead of going back to the room where his wife was, he went to where Monique was. He walked in to see her sitting in the bed holding their son who was squirming all around. He was not crying, but she was trying to comfort the little one.

"They kept asking me what his name is," she started calmly. "I told them I had to wait on his daddy." She took a cloth and wiped the baby's mouth.

"When did you have him?"

"About, um, 6:19 p.m." She diverted her attention to the clock across from the bed as if she needed a reminder.

"I've been here since 12," he said.

"Yeah, I figured when your phone was off that you were in court or with Yvonne."

"How was your labor?" Victor was still standing over her admiring the new life that she held in her arms.

"Pretty smooth, no problems. Here, meet your son," Monique offered him the baby. Victor felt that he was violating his family by holding on to another newborn, until the reality that the newborn was his dawned on him.

"Oh my goodness. He has some weight on him," Victor commented.

"8 pounds, 9 ounces," she replied beaming. She was so happy to see Victor there and owning up to his illegitimate newborn.

"Kalil."

"Kalil?"

"Yeah, Kalil."

"I was sort of hoping that we could name him Victor. Victor Russell II." Victor started laughing and looked at her like she was the biggest comedienne he had ever seen.

"Seriously," he said still laughing.

"I am," she was grinning from ear to ear. He had not seen a genuine smile on her lips in a long, long time. It seemed that their relationship had been understandably strained during the entire pregnancy.

"Monique, how in the hell am I gonna name him after me?"

"He's your son, isn't he?"

"Yeah, then what am I going to tell my wife when she wants to name our son after me?"

"Tell her she should have had a son first. The name is already taken," her attitude was starting to kick in.

"We need to name him and I think that Kalil is a good one. Doesn't he look like a Kalil?"

"I guess. He is going to have your last name though." Victor exhaled deeply. He knew that this was going to be a production. There was no way he could really fight fire with fire. In order for him to do that, he would have to come clean with Yvonne. Until he did that, Monique would have leverage on him. What was worse was that she knew it.

"Here you go," she slid the birth certificate over to him on the cart. He looked down at it.

"You spelled Kalil right," and he turned his attention back to the newborn.

"Sign your name."

"Monique."

"Sign your name."

"There will be time for that later, I am trying to spend time with my son."

"No, you will do it now." Monique was dead serious. She was not going to let him get away with putting it off. There need not be any confusion. Victor did not move fast enough for her. Monique got out of the bed and put her slippers on. She wrapped her robe around her and tied the belt.

"Where are you going?"

"To introduce myself to Mrs. Russell."

"Damn Monique! I'm owning up to my responsibility."

"No you aren't. Your wife has no idea that you have a whole other family and we're right here down the hall from her. She has a right to know."

"My wife is none of your business," his tongue was sharp and strong, "What we do has nothing to do with you. Lay your ass back in this bed. You and I will handle this matter about our son together. Just us!" Victor reluctantly signed the birth certificate. Even though Monique did not get the name she wanted, she got the signature.

Alicia showed up at Monique's house with a moving truck and a lover with his friends. Monique had been home with the baby for a little over a month and between feedings and naps, she managed to pack up her whole apartment. She took advantage of her friend's gang of associates to get her move done for free. Now she would have help with her bills and her child. Both ladies were happy to be rooming with each other.

Chapter 7

The adjustment period to having a roommate was not long at all. The women had been friends for so long, they practically already knew each other's ins and outs. The only difference was that now one of them had a child. Alicia was happy to have the company and Monique was glad to have the financial help.

Monique did not want to spoil Kalil, but she enjoyed spending the time with him that she could. Her job had given her 8 weeks and they were almost up. She was not looking forward to going back to work and leaving her prince with someone else. Monique was a bit thrown by how quickly she became attached to her baby. He clearly meant everything to her.

Little Kalil was just as precious as he wanted to be. It was hard to tell who he looked the most like. He had his mother's dark complexion and his father's sharp nose. He was a good mix. Despite all of the drama that was surrounding his life, he was a pretty happy baby. That was unless Victor came around. As soon as Kalil heard Victor's voice, he would begin to stir anxiously. Sometimes, he would even cry.

As much as Victor's feelings were hurt by this, Monique knew what that was attributed to. Almost the entire time that she was carrying him, her feelings for Victor wavered from love to bitter hatred. There were times when she would just sit and cry. The situation that she was in was not to be desired and she attributed that to him mostly. In her head, they were equal partners in this whole thing, but Victor was trying to skimp on his end of the deal.

It was not so much as Victor trying to get out of his responsibilities as a father, but he was a husband first. His legitimate family came before whatever he had going on the side. Monique knew this, but it was hard for her to deal with it. Especially recognizing that he did not have the balls to tell his wife about them yet. The disgruntled sentiment she had for Victor showed itself through their son.

True to his word, Victor did support Kalil financially. When his days were short at the office, no one was the wiser. He doted on his daughter and talked about how she was the love of his life. Early days at work meant more family time. Bowles and Laughton was big on family. Since this was their first child, no one could have ever suspected that he was splitting his time between two households.

Alicia gave Victor a fair shake. She felt that she had to since this man was going to be in and out of her place now that Monique was staying there. Just because she gave him a fair shake did not mean that she had to like him. Tolerate was more the word. They were cordial, not friendly. Victor could see why. He was living an out right lie to his wife of almost four years.

The majority of the time when Victor came, Alicia would stay off to herself in her room or just leave all together. The sister was not in the business of being fake. She did appreciate the money that he contributed to the household. No matter what, he always bought whatever groceries were on both Alicia and Monique's list. She had to give him a thumbs up for that.

He tried to spend time with Kalil at least twice a week. It was becoming a hard task to maneuver, but it was not Kalil's fault that he came into the world. Monique did not complain.

Yvonne was happy that the delivery had gone off without a hitch and her daughter was growing beautifully. She spent her days with not a care in the world. When Kalia cried, her mother was right there to soothe her. Kalia loved taking baths. She would just coo to her mother and splash the water as much as her little 2 month old hand could. Since it was just the two of them the majority of the time, the place she became the most accustomed to was Yvonne's lap.

Kalia looked like a dream come true. She had thick curly hair. Her eyes were happy and wide. Even though her father was the darker of her parents, when Yvonne held her it was hard to tell where Yvonne ended and Kalia began.

Victor told Yvonne that she was spoiling the girl rotten and Yvonne would sheepishly deny it. Then she would look over at Kalia and give her a wink. Kalia could not have come at a better time. Both of her parents were deep into their steady careers. Up until that point, the mortgage had been doubled up every month and they were not hurting for anything. The Russells were eating, good.

"How's the wittle baby, baby," Rosemary came to visit Yvonne. Being a relatively new mother herself, she knew firsthand what it was like to quit her job to be a mother full time.

"She's fine," Yvonne responded and Rosemary grabbed a hold of Kalia before crossing the threshold into the house.

"You know Yvonne, it's okay for you to come out walking more than twice a week." Rosemary jumped right into it, "Susan thinks you're weak." The ladies laughed. They all were in the same boat. They all were women who did not have to work because their husbands made enough to support their comfortable lifestyles. So they had to find things to do to keep themselves occupied.

"You heard me tell Susan that I have to work myself up to where you ladies are. I'm still recovering. Come here Jackson," Yvonne wanted to hold Rosemary's maturing little boy.

"Susan is harmless, she just needs some attention. Charles has been putting in some mean hours lately and she does not see him very much."

"I'm sure it's all for the good. It just means more money for her to spend in the end."

"They make plenty of that. He just hasn't been around very much lately," Rosemary sounded. It was impossible not to hear the disappointment in her voice. Her heart went out to her friend.

"Oh," Yvonne commented not really knowing what to say. Her husband was home a lot more now than before. His case load was a bit lighter than before, just in case Yvonne needed him if Kalia got sick. Of course there was no telling what the future held. She might be in the same scenario in the next year.

"Anyway, we're all having tea, us and the mommies from Lakeside down the street. We're going to Barbara's house. I know you haven't been to her house yet, but trust me, it'll put our little 5500 square foot homes to shame."

"Is it really that big?"

"Big and nice! Her mother-in-law bought her a pair of 2 carat, internally flawless, diamond studs when she gave birth to the twins."

"What?! That's insane!" Yvonne exclaimed.

"Tell me about it. Don't forget it, this Friday at 1." Rosemary scooped up her son, who was finding quite a nice home behind Yvonne's planter playing peek-a-boo. He loved that plant.

Yvonne did not mind entertaining her neighbors. They meant well. She enjoyed doing things with them, it helped her to keep her sanity. Both Rosemary and Susan had boys, so they had no experience with ear piercing.

Yvonne looked at her daughter and knew she was just itching to have some small studs in her ears. Luckily she was born with a head full of thick hair, which she inherited from her mother, but she was still missing something. Yvonne decided to take Kalia to get her ears pierced by herself. She and Victor agreed that they would go together, but Yvonne simply could not wait. She made a real production out of it. She drove all the way to Lenox Mall and strolled Kalia around. She was a proud new mommy.

Kalia was no stranger to the stroller, she was cool as long as they were moving. Yvonne figured out that if she rolled slowly that when she did stop, Kalia would not notice it right away, making her slower to cry. She figured out the tricks, but she had to prepare herself for the shrieking cry that her daughter was going to let out when the piercing gun penetrated those precious ears. For a first time mother, her eyes watered thinking about the pain that she was causing her daughter.

After the piercing, Kalia looked at her mother like she was the world's worst. Yvonne was thankful to the suggestions for both attendants to pierce her ears simultaneously, so Kalia would not have an opportunity squirm around when the second ear was pierced. After she experienced the pain from the first piercing, it would have certainly been a fight to get to the second.

As any mother would, Yvonne was there to console and rock her daughter to calmness after the shock. It took some time, too. From the time they left the store until they got back out to the parking lot, Kalia whimpered in pain. She rolled her little head from side to side trying to find a comfortable way to lay. Once they were in the car, Yvonne turned on some of the same relaxing music that she used on Victor and it lulled her to sleep.

Yvonne was careful not to make any sudden stops or drive recklessly so she would not disturb her princess. Heading down 75/85 south, she was driving in the last two lanes, for the slower traffic, taking her dear time getting home. She got into the lane to the left of her so the oncoming traffic could make a nice transition into the highway speed. There was a burgundy Infiniti that was speeding up the on ramp, flying like a bat out of hell.

When the car passed her, she made a point to look at the driver who was not thinking about any body else's life, not even his own. It was Victor. She could not figure out where he was coming from. He was getting on at a place where she did not know that he had any business. She called him on her cell phone.

"Victor, where are you?"

"Just leaving the office."

"Hey Honey, you just flew past me on the interstate," she said in a puzzled voice.

"What? Oh...where...I see you," he looked in his rearview mirror. "Hey Baby!" He sounded excited. He was glad that she could not see his face.

"Where are you coming from?"

"Oh, uh...I was actually on my way home," he was speaking slowly, "and I was running out of gas, so I had to just stop where I could."

"Okay well, we're behind you. I just wanted to let you know that we were back here."

"Where are you coming from?" He knew that she could not be doing any dirt, she had Kalia with her. He was very nervous. Victor was not worried about her finding out that he had just kissed his child that she knew nothing about goodbye. He was uneasy because even in this huge metropolis, he managed to run into his wife in a place where he was not necessarily supposed to be.

"We went to get Kalia's ears pierced."

"Yvonne, you were supposed to wait until this weekend so I could go with you." His voice showed disappointment.

"I know, I couldn't wait and neither could she. She asked me this morning when she got up if I would take her."

"Alright, meet you at the house," he signed off. She felt better about it after she talked to him. She believed him when he told her that he had to get off of the interstate to get gas. Why would her husband lie?

Victor had been keeping up his façade for almost a year. The affair had been going on for much longer than that, but now there was the additional family. Yvonne had really thrown him for a loop. He turned off the radio in his car his mind needed to be clear. He had gone to see Monique and hold their love/lust child in his very arms. He wondered how much longer was this going to pan out in his favor. This secret was eating him up and every time that he looked into Yvonne's eyes, it was just too much for him to come right out to tell her.

Monique began to notice that Kalil was urinating twice as much as normal. Really, it was Victor who observed how quickly he was going through pampers. Monique, being a first time mother thought that it was okay. Victor knew from experiences with Kalia that healthy patterns did not change that drastically. Monique thought that he was too young to have a urinary tract infection, which was the first thing that came to mind when Victor started stressing it.

Ultimately, it was his mother's decision whether or not, she wanted to get him checked out. She opted to wait a few more days to see if he cleared up and got back to normal. She cleaned up his diet and made sure not to feed him anything that he was not accustomed to eating. Recently, Monique introduced peaches into his diet. She thought that it might be an allergy. When Kalil had blood in his urine, she said enough is enough and he needed to go to the doctor.

Victor was very surprised when he got the call saying that Monique was taking little Kalil to the hospital to be checked out. He told her that he would sit on top of his phone until she called. One hour later, Monique had shown up at the Crawford Long emergency room. By the time they got Kalil back to see a doctor, Victor had already called twice. He was very concerned. She was touched.

The physician asked Monique a series of questions to get a history on what was going on. He could understand how bloody urine could cause alarm. He took Kalil in his arms and set him on the table. The doctor took his hands and gently pressed on Kalil's abdomen and back.

"What?" Monique asked when she saw the way the doctor looked when touching his back.

"Nothing, I'm trying to concentrate," he lied not wanting to alarm her any further.

"Do you think you know what it is?"

"We're going to run some tests. I'll send a nurse in a minute," he said and walked out of the room. Monique looked at her son and began to cry. A few sparing tears crawled down her cheeks. She had no idea what was going on with him. The doctor had, so far, shed no light on what it could be.

A few minutes later, a nurse walked in. She drew a few small vials of blood. The nurse enlisted the help of Monique to keep a bubbly Kalil from moving. Just for good measure, the doctor ordered an ultrasound. After an hour of waiting, the nurse came back and told Monique that the blood work showed nothing alarming and they were going to do further testing.

"Dr. Anderson is the pediatrician that your son needs to see," the nurse explained.

"Where is he?" Monique had grown impatient, she demanded answers.

"He is in emergency surgery right now. He is the one who will review the test results and ultrasound."

"We'll wait."

"Ms. Crenshaw," the nurse double checked her name, "the process takes a few days. We can't find anything in the preliminary results that puts your son in imminent danger. Here is a number for you to call if you don't hear from Dr. Anderson in 10 business days."

Monique reluctantly gathered her belongings and prepared to leave. She had gone to the emergency room seeking answers. Instead, she got no resolution. The nurse told her to wait 10 whole business days. She knew that she was going to drive herself crazy waiting the time out.

Feeling a small bit of relief, Monique called Victor as soon as she buckled Kalil in the car. The call took some of the edge off of both of them. It meant a lot to talk to Victor and know that he was behind her. They were both still very concerned about their child. Victor was restless, he told Monique that he would meet her at Alicia's place.

He arrived shortly after she did and gave her a big hug and kiss. He held Kalil in his arms the entire time that he was there. Kalil was, as usual, agitated by his father, but Victor was not going to put him down and that was all there was to it. Eventually, the little one settled down.

Monique was going to be careful not to introduce him to any new foods. Baby chicken, peas and corn were his favorites. He seemed to like the peaches and Monique was holding on to her hopes that somehow the urine problem was related to a food allergy. Victor's phone rang and he wanted to ignore it, but he could not. It was Yvonne.

"Hello," he said knowing how Monique got when he talked to his wife.

"Hey Baby," Yvonne replied sweetly. "I just called the office, where are you?"

"I'm down at Sparky's," he lied. Monique shot him a nasty look.

"It's awfully quiet down there."

"I'm in the car, I had to get something for Sonya."

"Tell her we said hi." Yvonne wore out her 'we' speaking of herself and Kalia. She was ecstatic being a mother.

"I will. I'll be leaving here any minute."

"Ok, I have something for you. Hurry home." He could hear Kalia making all kinds of baby noises in the background. Hearing her voice tugged at his heart strings.

"When are you going to tell her Victor?" Monique started up.

"Look, I already told you that what goes on with me and my wife is between us."

"Are you saying that it has nothing to do with me?"

"That's what I'm saying."

"Victor, we have not been intimate in several months, but that does not disregard that fact that we were."

"So what Nique? The sex is over," they could hear the front door slam. That was Alicia's way of telling them that she did not want to hear it. She had left.

"And...you are still a part of my life. We are a part of each other's lives."

"Well you know what, there are other things that we need to be worried about right now. Our son is sick! Maybe you missed that."

"How could I miss it Victor," her tone had raised to match his. "How could I miss it when I was just at the emergency room all by my damn self? How can I miss it when I only see you twice a week and I know that when you leave you're going home to her?" Monique pointed to his cell phone indicating Yvonne.

"I know you are doing the best you can." He tried to give her credit.

"The best I can alone."

"Nique you talk about me like I'm a deadbeat father. I come by, I see him, I spend time with him, I give you money and might I add, I buy groceries for the whole house!"

"Until the day that you can take Kalil to your house, you will be a deadbeat!"

"Don't hold your breath," Victor commented a tad more calm.

"Are you saying that you are not going to tell your wife that you have another child out here?" Her face was twisted in disbelief.

"I will."

"Victor you've been saying that since I told you I was pregnant!" Monique was screaming, she was positively irate.

"I told you I would!" His yelling was no equal counterpart.

"Our child is going on 6 months old! This thing between us is not new to the block! I can't believe that you have managed to keep it from her all this time! Victor I feel like you don't love your child at all!"

"I love both of my children, in case you couldn't tell. I'm sorry that I can't drop what I'm doing every minute of my life to help you or to be there for you. I told you in the beginning not to have this child."

"Oh, so we're back on that now?" She had an inflection in her voice. "I knew that I hadn't heard the end of it."

"We're not back on it, I just had to reiterate that you chose to be a single mother."

"You are disrespecting me in my house! How dare you say that?"

"Nique, alright, tell me again that I gave you money for an abortion. Tell me that I told you how less complicated everybody's life would be."

"Tell me, Victor that you kept your word and went to the clinic with me. Tell me that you were trying to salvage your own pathetic life!"

"Yeah, I may have had my own selfish reasons, but you can't sit here and make me believe that you did not see where this was headed. Even in marriages children add a difficult element." Kalil began to cry.

"See, you made my baby cry you bastard." Monique took him from Victor's arms and started pacing back and forth.

"The point of the matter is, Nique, this whole thing could have been prevented. Since we didn't, we have to deal with the choices that we made. The timing just isn't right, right now."

"When will it be right, at Kalil's high school graduation, or when he haphazardly meets Kalia and they start dating? I don't know what your problem is but soon enough you are going to have to face the music."

"I know."

"Maybe I'll tell her myself." In one swift move, Victor jumped up and put his hand around Monique's neck.

"I'm tired of your damn threats," he was so close to her that she could feel his breath on her face. His tone was very low. "You won't get too many more times to use them. You hear me?" There was no response. Monique was looking at him with her eyes popping out of her head. She was holding on to Kalil like her life depended on it.

Victor knew he had to get out of that house before he did something crazy. He turned and stormed out. He left Monique freaking out, she had never seen him like that before. He totally flipped the script on her. She called his bluff one too many times. Kalil was restless the whole night. Crying just for being unhappy. Crying for his mother who was, herself, suffering internally.

He needed another nature escape. He took a deep breath. Since there was no way he could just call in sick to life with two infants and a full time job of supporting them both, he imagined that he was back there. Another deep breath. He put his mind in a happy place. There was no other choice, if he came clean with Yvonne tonight, after fighting with Monique, it was not going to be pretty.

Another deep breath. His mind ventured into worry about Kalil. Victor prayed that whatever was ailing him was not serious and that he would recover soon. He knew the stress from Monique worrying about Kalil was part of what really set her off. Another deep breath. His mind ventured to the conversation that he had with his wife. She said that she had something for him.

Please don't let her come to the door in a negligee, he thought. He was not in the mood for sex. He blasted Outkast, *Aquemini*. The album was an old favorite, a classic. There was a nice blend of raps, on top of funky beats and grown men singing melodies. He coasted all the way home.

He arrived home and he could hear Yvonne laughing as he walked in. If she was watching T.V. then the surprise was not a romantic one. He relaxed a little more. She jumped up when she heard the beeping from the alarm, signaling that one of the doors was open.

"Baby," she squealed obviously eager to show him his surprise.

"Baby," he mocked her and she hit his arm. Just seeing her face relieved him a bit.

"Shut up. I'm excited to see you even if you don't feel the same way," she said and turned to walk away. He followed her, grabbing her by the waist and looking her in the eyes.

"I am very happy to see you."

"Come over here, my show is on." She directed him towards the couch.

"Yvonne, you go through so much trouble." He commented seeing a bag with tissue paper coming out of the top.

"Look, it's the little things in life, okay. I like doing for others. You know my history and you know that I don't have many people dear to me. You and Kalia are my family. All she wants is a dry diaper and a full stomach. She could care less about the rest," Yvonne said playfully. She kissed Kalia on her forehead and Kalia bounced around her walker. She loved to sit in it.

"You're right Baby, thank you."

"Open it," she advised. She was bubbling over waiting for him to dig into the bag. He looked at her and saw the vibrance on her face. Whatever was in the bag was eating her up for Victor to see it. He stopped pushing aside the tissue paper and stared at her.

"Victor!" She yelled knowing exactly what he was doing. Stall tactic, he was making her wait. He burst out laughing then tore into the bag. There were a pair of new chocolate brown leather Gucci loafers.

"Wow," he said and left his mouth hanging open while he inspected them.

"You're wondering why, even a Gucci connoisseur such as yourself has never seen those. My love, that's because they just came out. I had to get them before you saw them or else it wouldn't have been special."

"Yes it would have."

"No, because then you would have been asking me to pick them up for you instead of them being a surprise."

"Yvonne, I love these! I am so impressed." She could see that he was genuinely surprised.

"I know," she said smartly and walked into her home office. Victor ran behind her and hugged her.

"Thank you so much." He said and lifted her by her waist onto the desk. He sat down in the computer chair and kissed her up her soft, golden thighs. She giggled and tried to push him away from her. It did not work. He kissed down her left leg all the way to her feet. Slowly, painstakingly, he moved his lips back up her left leg and down her right. He held her tenderly and continued to kiss up her right leg. Victor pulled her shorts off. With the help of his hands, she parted her legs and he used his mouth to stimulate her.

His tongue found its way to the center of her body and she spread her legs further. Hungrily he found the place where she wanted him to be. Pleasing her excited him so that he began to want her more and more. Sensing his need, she slid off of the desk and pushed the chair back slightly. He stood up and she undid his belt and let his pants fall to the ground.

Yvonne pushed him back down and sat on his lap. She sensually nibbled at his ears lobes. He maneuvered his head around to meet hers and kissed her, probing his tongue down her throat. She inserted him inside of her and started to rock slowly back and forth. They kissed and held each other tightly. Victor pulled off her shirt and unhooked her bra. He wanted to see all of her. Touch her, taste her.

She leaned back and used the desk for support while still moving her hips slowly back and forth. Her husband cupped her breasts and alternated putting them in his mouth. She felt so good. There was nothing but love between them. Pure emotion, pure desire. Yvonne was his cure to dealing with the entire outside world. When he was with her, she made everything alright. Her rocking began to speed up. It was still slow, but just a little bit faster. She was taking him there.

Nothing else mattered at that moment. They had no worries and everything was okay. Victor felt himself welling up, with emotion and satiety. He could never explain why he had done the things that he had to her. He betrayed their union and his wife's trust. He was all that she had, the only person she could depend on. He knew that if Yvonne had one inkling of the truth, she would not be passionately making love to him. She would not have gifted him.

It took all he had to hold back what he was feeling. His eyes watered. He closed them so she could not see. Yvonne was reaching her peak. She was so in love with her husband. No other man meant more to her, nor could come between them.

When they came to a calming place, he buried his head in her chest so she would not see his eyes. He knew that if she looked at him in his eyes, the tears would fall. He just sat there, holding her. She could sense the emotion, but took it for pure love. She felt in her heart that her husband adored her the same way she did him. She held on to him. They sat there in the office holding on to the warmth of their existence.

"Bowles and Laughton Attorneys-At-Law. How may I direct your call?"

"Hello, may I speak to Victor Russell?" A female asked in a dignified nature.

"Victor Russell is in court all day today, is there a message?" Ms. Betsy answered the call.

"Yes, this is Kim Barnes with Dr. Anderson's office at Crawford Long Hospital. Could you please have him call me. It's regarding Kalia."

"Kalia, yes...his daughter." Ms. Betsy's voice sounded concerned.

"He needs to make an appointment to get her test results back. We can't give them over the phone."

"Did you try calling his wife?"

"Ma'am, this is the only number that I have." Ms. Betsy thought that was rather strange.

"Give me your number Ms. Barnes."

"Okay, my number here is..." the lady called out the number to Dr. Anderson's office.

Ms. Betsy began to fret. Victor had not mentioned anything about Kalia being sick and here a nurse was calling with some test results. The more time passed, the more Ms. Betsy began to worry. She wondered why the nurse could not reach Yvonne. Yvonne rarely left the house, she should have been there. The older lady picked up the phone to dial.

"Yvonne," she said.

"Yes ma'am, is Victor okay?" Yvonne was wondering why his secretary would be calling her in the middle of the day.

"He's fine, you know he's in court today, right?"

"Sure that's what he told me."

"Well, Kim Barnes just called and left a message with me."

"Who is Kim Barnes?"

"Why, she just called and said something about Kalia. She works at Crawford Long and left the number to Dr. Anderson's office."

"She was born there, but her last check up turned out fine." Yvonne commented.

"I thought she had been born there. I don't know, Yvonne. She left a number and said to give it to Victor to set up an appointment for test results."

"What is it?" Yvonne, being a business woman, had pen and paper by the phone. She jotted the number down and thanked Ms. Betsy.

Yvonne called the number and the secretary told her Dr. Anderson had just gotten with a patient and scheduled a meeting with her. Yvonne was still puzzled, Kalia had not taken any tests. She decided not to say anything to Victor because she was sure it was all just a mix up and did not want to falsely concern him.

Chapter 8

"Hi, we're here to see Dr. Anderson. A nurse called yesterday saying something about test results. We have an appointment at 1."

"Mrs. Russell?"

"Yes."

"Have a seat, he'll call for you in a moment." Yvonne had been mulling over how she would tell them that it had to be a mistake. Her daughter had not been tested for anything and she had no idea how her husband's name got mixed up in the whole thing. The wait was not long at all.

"Mrs. Russell," he called out. Dr. Anderson was a tall man with a gentle, clean shaven face. All of his hair was silver. Carefully, Yvonne got up and gathered her things. Kalia was asleep and her mother had a blanket over her.

"I am," she extended her hand.

"Dr. Anderson, how are you?" They exchanged firm handshakes.

"Fine."

"Good, come this way." He led the way to the office.

"How did you know that the results were back?"

"Sir, I got a call from a nurse named Kim Barnes."

"There is no Kim Barnes in my office."

"That's who called my husband's job. She left a message with his secretary, Ms. Betsy who, in turn, called me."

"Maybe Ms. Betsy got the name wrong. Your case was given to me by the E.R. It seems that your child has what appears to be an extremely rare genetic disease. The initial blood work did not show any evidence of this because a primary blood test won't show it."

"During the testing," he continued, "they also did an ultrasound, just in case the blood work did not yield any clues. In the ultrasound, we found what appear to be cysts in the kidney. The disease is called polycystic kidney disorder or PKD.

"Dr. Anderson, I have not taken Kalia to the E.R. The last check-up she had a month ago came out fine. I don't understand any of this. I think your wires are crossed." He looked at her over his wire framed glasses and appeared to be puzzled. He had just gone through the motions of describing to this woman what was happening wrong with her child and she was saying that it was not her child.

"I have here," he fumbled with the papers in the file, "a number 404-555-1213 for your home that was found to be disconnected."

"That is not my number."

"You said that we called your husband, Victor Russell?"

"You did."

"You have no idea what I'm talking about?"

"No, sir."

"You child's name is Kalil Russell?"

"Kalia. K-a-l-i-a...Russell." She added the last name with hesitation.

"Does your husband have any other children?"

"No," she laughed. "You see, there's some kind of mistake."

"When was the last time that you came to the E.R.?"

"When I was in labor over 6 months ago." Yvonne was very certain that there was something wrong with the filing system. There was no way she was that clueless about her daughter. If Kalia was sick, her mother certainly would have known about it.

"Give me a second," Dr. Anderson excused himself. He went to the records section of the office. He was baffled, he did not see how there was any way that their staff could have messed up and called the wrong patient. He told one of his medical filers to look into the situation. At this point, there was a father in common and a name that was too similar for comfort.

Dr. Anderson went back to his office to tell Mrs. Russell what was going on. He did not want her to be in the dark or feel that she was forgotten about. He tried to explain to her that it would probably take some time to figure out where and how the mix up occurred. In that time, Kalia stirred just a little, she was sound asleep. Yvonne hoped that the staff got to the bottom of it all so she could get on with her life.

Once everything got all figured out, she would tell Victor and they would both laugh about the blooper. Of course by then, the real parents would have been alerted. She thanked God that it was not her baby girl and then tried to put herself in their shoes. They have a sick child and do not know it. She imagined an anxious mother sitting by the phone, desperately curious as to what was going on with her child. She pictured a seemingly healthy child who all of a sudden fell ill.

Yvonne knew that lots of times, parents want to blame themselves for the things that happen to their children. They feel like it must be God repaying them for some sin from days passed. She could not envision the pain that they would experience. Dr. Anderson did say that it was a rare disease, her mind blocked out the rest because it did not concern Kalia. She had known all along that the news was mistaken.

With the disease being a rare one, that probably meant that modern science did not know much about it or there was not a cure. Those poor parents would more than likely be facing the loss of their child. Yvonne's mind was in left field, looking down at her perfectly healthy child and hearing the disturbing news about someone else's.

"Ok Mrs. Russell, this is what we have come up with. Your daughter, Kalia Russell was born on March 9th correct?"

"Yes." That was one of the few things they had right.

"There was a boy, Kalil, K-a-l-i-l Russell was also born on March 9th, here at Crawford Long. Somehow, your husband's name was put on the records for both children. There must have been a mix up. Honestly, I do not understand how this could have happened. We usually don't make inaccuracies like that."

"Mistakes happen, we're all human." Yvonne responded light-heartedly about it.

"Well Mrs. Russell," the doctor stood up to send her on her way.

"Yvonne," she corrected him.

"Yvonne, thank you for your patience and understanding. Hopefully, we can get to the bottom of this and soon. The only working number on the file is your husband's work number. We have to find these parents." He extended his hand.

"Thank you very much Dr. Anderson."

"I'm glad to tell you that your daughter has healthy kidneys." They both laughed. Dr. Anderson's laugh was nervous laughter because he was realizing the magnitude of what had just happened. Unless the parents of Kalil called the hospital, they would not know that their child had such a debilitating disease. Yvonne was laughing because she and her family were officially in the clear.

After she left the hospital, she headed over to Victor's job. It was mid day and she hoped that he had a minute to see his family. He normally did not schedule clients back to back, so if he was with anyone, then she could wait. Arriving, she parked in the space set aside for visitors and did not bother getting out the stroller. The visit would be short.

Yvonne spotted Ms. Betsy first. The first thing out of the secretary's mouth was asking how the baby was doing? Yvonne knew she was concerned about the message that had been relayed. Yvonne told Ms. Betsy that there had been some kind of mistake.

Ms. Betsy oohed and ahhed over Kalia. Kalia loved the attention. Other lawyers were tipping their head to Yvonne and the female paralegals wanted to see Victor's spawn. Kalia was decked out from head to toe. Her mother was not doing bad either. They both were wearing pink. Kalia had on a cute cotton pink and white jumper with bees on it. Her mother put a matching pink headband on her. Yvonne, on the other hand, was wearing white business slacks with pink and black stripes on them. Her shirt was crisp white and her accessories were pink.

Ms. Betsy thought that Yvonne was early for an appointment, but when she realized that Yvonne had not talked to Victor before coming, Ms. Betsy said that he was not in his office.

"I come all the way down here and he's not here. Is he in court?" Yvonne asked with her hands on her hips, looking down at Kalia bouncing up and down on Ms. Betsy's lap.

"No Yvonne, I don't know where he is. He's been gone for quite some time."

"A long lunch, huh?"

"I guess so." Yvonne was starting to feel like her husband was hiding something from her. There was the strange incident on the highway, several times she called and he was not at the office or in court. It just was not like him to not be where he was supposed to be.

She tried to brush it off and made it home safely with her prized package. When she arrived home, she went over to Rosemary's house. Rosemary was taking a break, she had just set Jackson down for a nap.

"Hello Yvonne, aren't the two of your cute today?"

"Thank you, we had an appointment at the hospital today."

"Is everything okay?" Rosemary sounded concerned.

"With us, at least I think."

"What do you mean you think."

"Well, yesterday the hospital called Victor's job and left a message about some results to a test, his secretary called me and I made an appointment to get the results back today. The problem is, Kalia has not taken any test. All of her check-ups have been fine."

"So there must have been some kind of mix up."

"Yeah, that's what Dr. Anderson said."

"Ooh, I've heard good things about Dr. Anderson, he's an awesome pediatrician. If your baby gets sick, you want Dr. Anderson to be her doctor."

"His bedside manner really caught my attention. He told me there was another child who had been born there with a name very similar to Kalia's with Victor's name down as the father. They were born on the same day."

"I don't know how that happened."

"Me either, but I'm worried now. I think I want to have Kalia tested for the disease anyway."

"What was it?" Rosemary was being nosey.

"Some kind of kidney disease."

"Oh those poor parents," Rosemary put her hand over her heart.

"I know. I'm worried just a bit."

"You shouldn't be. If Dr. Anderson did not recommend that you have her tested, then don't worry about it. You're just being a new mother," Rosemary teased, shooing Yvonne with her hand. "Kalia is perfectly healthy." Yvonne appreciated the vote of confidence. She really needed it right about then. The ladies sat there and talked for a minute longer, then Yvonne went home to give her neighbor more resting time before Jumping Jackson came into consciousness.

That night, Yvonne did not sleep well, nor did Victor. They were alternately up and down all night. Yvonne's mind was going between feeling bad for those unknowing parents and speculating how her husband's name got on that file. Rosemary had done a pretty good job of calming her down for the time being. Hopefully, she would not really feel the need to have Kalia tested.

Victor felt that his only real place of refuge was at the office. There, he was on neutral ground. Either one,

Yvonne or Monique could comfortably reach him there. Monique still had not heard anything from the doctor's office. He was trying to wait patiently. Everyday that passed, he was that much closer to telling her to go back up there and see what was taking so long. If anything happened to Kalil, Monique would never forgive Victor. She would eternally blame him for not being there, it would get messy and he knew it. All hell would break loose.

Kalia started to cry about 1:30 that night. They both jumped up, but Victor told Yvonne to go back to sleep. He picked her up and went to fix her a bottle. He fed it to her, watching late night T.V. After he burped and changed her, he stretched out on the couch and put her on his chest.

He loved to feel her heart beat through her small chest. It was so much faster than his. Even after 6 months, he was still in awe of her tiny hands and feet. He loved to feel her squirm around in his arms. To him, it just represented life and vitality. Everything that Kalia was and did, he was completely smitten with. Victor would give his left arm to protect her. He gently rubbed her back, relaxing her and letting her know that daddy was there.

Yvonne slipped behind them, kissed Victor on the forehead and patted Kalia's back. The little princess was slipping further into sleep. She went into her office and got on the internet. She was not looking up anything in particular, the bedroom was a dark, restless box. After all, she had nothing to do the next day. She contemplated the thought that the test was an old one and the results just resurfaced. If they could transpose her husband as someone else's father, they could loose test results.

Sonya was pleasantly surprised to see Victor. Since he was caught between two infant children, he had not been around as much as usual. She understood. She was happy that her old friend still had time to come to Sparky's to pay her a visit.

"I lied on you the other day," he started out. He was dressed in olive green suit pants and an off-white starched cotton button down with a loosened tie.

"How did you lie on me Victor?"

"Yvonne called me when I was at Monique's house. I told her I was here with you and she told me to tell you hello for her."

"You didn't lie on me, you lied on yourself," she spoke. With the mere flicker of her tongue, Victor was mesmerized. She was the eye in his hurricane.

"I guess."

"So what you're telling me is, Yvonne still doesn't know." Sonya put a coaster down on the bar and a Hennessy on top. Victor immediately rested his hand around the glass.

"Right."

"Victor, you need to be ashamed of yourself," she laughed. "How old are the kids?"

"Going on 7 months now."

"So you have managed to hide an affair, another pregnancy and a child from your wife?" She was in total shock thinking about the magnitude of it all.

"I'm not proud of it." She could tell that he was being truthful. He could not even look her in the eye as he told her.

"That's an awesome feat. I don't see how you managed to do all of that. Especially if Monique is as feisty as you say she is. I'm surprised she hasn't blown up your spot yet." Sonya flinched to get the dreds out of her eye.

"Believe me, she is on the verge. She just can't wait to expose me."

"I don't blame her. Of course, what she doesn't see is that won't make you want her any more than you do."

"Or don't. I wish her ass would just walk out of my life. Then there's Kalil. I don't want to give him up."

"I have to commend you for at least taking care of him."

"In this day of DNA uncoding. I didn't think I had a choice."

"There are a lot of guys who deny, deny, deny. They won't even take a paternity test. They just come up missing."

"Yeah, I hear the stories."

"I'm sure you do in your line of work."

"I don't want me and my wife to end up like that, divorced. I want up to be able to work through this. She is so good to me, Sonya. I don't have to ask for anything."

"I know. If you'd told her in the beginning, it would have hit her hard, but you may have been able to regroup. Now, so much time as passed, I'm not so sure that telling her would be the best thing to do. Well, on second thought," she looked up at the ceiling, "the sooner the better. Yvonne doesn't want to think that you have been keeping secrets for years. She'll never trust you again, never."

"That's what I'm afraid of."

"Ooh, boy, you have gotten yourself knee deep in it!" Sonya sounded like she was singing Victor's blues.

"Tell me about it. Hit me again." She poured him another drink.

"Look at me, alone with my son. There's no man around. His dad walked out one day and I don't even know where he is. Now, how am I supposed to teach him how to be a man? Victor, you gotta stop being selfish. Put yourself in Yvonne's shoes." He sat there thinking for a minute. Sonya slipped away and filled a few orders.

"Her shoes," he said matter-of-factly.

"How would you feel if you found out that she was having an affair on you? Think of how she quit work and you are supporting her and Kalia. Now imagine that she doesn't cook for you or support you emotionally. There was no trip to the mountains, because she didn't care enough to notice your depressed state. She's sharing the most sacred parts of her with a man that she did not keep her vow to love or cherish or support for the rest of her life. Imagine that she is not your rib."

Victor damn near started crying. He was taken back to the love making session they had in the office the night she surprised him with the shoes. Victor's heart was broken for causing her the pain that she had no knowledge of yet. He was already doubting himself as a man.

"If she weren't such a good wife..."

"But she is and you can't take that away."

"It all started innocent enough."

"An affair is never innocent." Sonya was going to bat for Yvonne. Victor could by no means give a reason that carried enough merit to cover up his actions. He treated Monique like crap because he had a queen at home, but due to the outside relationship, he was ultimately treating his queen like a pauper.

"Sonya, what should I do?"

"You are going to have to tell her. It won't be easy, be prepared for some broken dishes and your plasma will be in pieces on the floor. Maybe if you come out with things now, you can salvage your marriage. It will be hard and it will take some time, but it's better now than years down the road. Somehow, I don't think that Monique will be quiet that long."

"Me either, she caught a fit when Yvonne called and I lied about being here."

"That girl wants her presence felt." She was giving Victor tough love. Sonya was right. Monique wanted her presence felt. If she could not hurt Yvonne by taking her man, then she would hurt her by sharing him. Monique wanted Yvonne to know that she was there and had been there all along.

Monique had her calendar marked at 10 days. She still had a few boxes before she could call the hospital. In the meantime, Kalil was suffering. It did not appear that he was in much pain. He was sleeping and eating on schedule. The blood subsided a bit. It was not in all of his diapers, which eased her mind a bit. Unless it got worse between now and the 10th day, she would not be overly concerned.

Her worry was still evident every time that she was in Victor's ear. She knew that if his mind was consumed enough, that he would not be able to fully function. Since he could not be there enduring the sickness with her, she wanted him to be anguished with sleepless nights and torturously long work days. The way that she saw it, the more time Victor spent away from her and Kalil, the more time he spent with Yvonne and Kalia.

It pained her in the middle of the night to hear her son crying and know that she was the only one who could get him. She hated Yvonne for not working and sharing her parenting responsibilities. On Monique's end, it was all her, with the exceptionally small blocks of time that Victor could steal away.

She did not see why it was fair that Victor had not been open and honest with his wife who was living a fairytale only 20 minutes away. It was all too fresh for her to pick herself up and comprehend that Victor was going to be teaching her son bad values. Her eyes had tunnel vision.

Alicia's opinion did not matter. She tried to convince her friend that none of this had anything to do with Yvonne and that Monique should not have those feelings toward the innocent party in the triangle. It was not Yvonne's fault that she met Victor first. Then, she put it to her nicely. Would you rather be the one who is clueless or the one who knows?

Monique needed Alicia for her dose of realism. When the affair started, Alicia would tell her not to. She told her what problems it could lead to. All Monique was looking for then was a hand out. She wanted to have a connect in her industry for possible promotions or coercion when it came time for permanent job placement. As almost always, the sex became emotional.

Now, Alicia was mainly an ear and knowing Monique like she did, she knew that the girl would do whatever she wanted. Alicia still held true to her friend roots and gave a peace of her mind, only when she was asked. When she did speak, it was all reality. Monique did not want to hear it, but Alicia knew that she needed to. That's what friends are for.

Chapter 9

Unbeknownst to Yvonne, Victor had made arrangements to take Kalia to Rosemary's house so they could have a nice night out on the town. He called her from work and told her not to bother herself with cooking. She thought he was just going to bring home a pizza or some fast food. He showed up at the door, with Rosemary in tow and a dozen orange gerbera daisies.

Instead of him using his key, he rang the doorbell and stood so that Yvonne could only see Rosemary when she looked through the peephole. Pleasantly surprised to see Rosemary at her door that late in the afternoon, she opened it and Victor slid in front of their neighbor. Yvonne started laughing and put her hands over her mouth when she saw her husband presenting her with a hand full of flowers.

"Baby?"

"We are going on a date. Go get ready and I will get a bag for Kalia. We have 20 minutes before we have to leave." Yvonne wasted no time running to get ready. A short time later, she came down the stairs in a knee length, Bohemian skirt, various shades of brown, a white tank top and a cropped dark brown eyelet jacket. Her sandals and belt were also dark brown with gold accents. She put her hair in a big bun on the side of the back of her head and donned some huge gold dangle earrings.

She knew that Victor was going to love her outfit. He loved when she dressed like that, it was more of a carefree look. He felt that it made her look younger than she already was. Victor was already dressed in khaki slacks and a button down.

"You look beautiful," he said sincerely.

"Why thank you," she replied noticing that he found a vase to put her daisies in. They were on the island in the kitchen, simply gorgeous.

"Are you ready to go?"

"Where are we going?"

"Yvonne, you don't trust me?"

"No. I was watching an episode on T.V. where a man took his wife out for a nice fancy dinner and then he arranged to have her murdered when they were on the way to the car afterwards."

"Girl, you watch too much of that forensic stuff." He laughed easily.

"Ahh, what else am I supposed to do when Kalia is down for a nap? Those shows are so captivating, they just draw you right in."

"I guess we need to get you back to work, huh?"

"I trust you," she piped down. He reached over to grab her hand. They held hands all the way to the restaurant. It turned out that there was a new steakhouse that Victor wanted to try. Yvonne had never heard of it, having only been open a few months.

"Hello, I have a reservation for Victor Russell," he spoke to the maitre'd. Yvonne looked at him suspiciously.

"I told you about what I saw on the show," she whispered. "This is preplanned." Victor pinched her. The maitre'd was in a slate grey suit accented by a grey and maroon checkered tie. He was a little sweet or very, very metro sexual with slight spikes in his hair and slacks on the tight side.

"Hmm," he said skimming over the list, "oh yes, Mr. Russell. Right this way. I'll have Robin here escort you to your table." He spoke with a lisp. Yvonne wanted to burst out laughing and Victor could sense it. He knew better than to look at her, if he did, they would both be on the ground rolling. They were escorted to a circular booth in the rear of the restaurant.

"Baby," Yvonne started.

"Stop," Victor said. He knew that she was about to get going about the maitre'd.

"What I was about to say," she snickered, "is that I am impressed with this place. Where did you hear about it?" She had to come up with something else quickly.

"Don't worry about all that." A waiter came and greeted them. He brought with him a bottle of wine that was chilling on ice, also, waters with lemon. Then the waiter disappeared without taking their dinner orders.

"That's strange, he didn't bring us menus." The waiter returned with an hors devours plate of imported cheeses spread in a circle and lightly toasted bread. He poured wine into the goblets and presented the drinks to them before disappearing again.

"Yvonne, I am bringing you here today so that we can celebrate our anniversary."

"But, our anniversary is not for another three weeks."

"I know, I thought that whatever I did on that day, you would expect it. This is an early treat. Your entire meal has been preordered. You have nothing to worry about." Yvonne's mouth was wide open.

"The whole meal?"

"Yes, Baby, I'm gonna take care of you."

"Oh my goodness. Baby, thank you." Yvonne put her hand over her heart then leaned over to give him a smack on the lips. It was deeply heart felt and he knew it. Now, she really took the place in. The lights were dim, there was a candle on every table. She could hear mellow music creeping from the overhead speakers. She glanced around to see that most of the patrons there were so engrossed in who they were with, that they were not paying attention to the people around them. The aroma of flavor was heavy in the air. The first course came.

"For the lady," the waiter said placing a Caesar salad with shaved parmesan cheese and homemade croutons in front of Yvonne.

"For you sir," the waiter put Victor's Manhattan clam chowder soup and crackers in front of him.

"Victor, this is really sweet. Where did you get the idea to do this?"

"Does that really matter? No it doesn't, now sit back and enjoy your first course."

"How many courses are there?"

"I don't remember. I just know that you better eat every damn crumb because I'm paying big money for them. Every piece of ice, every herb," he joked.

"Shut up. So how was your day?"

"Just fine I couldn't wait to see your face. You always do so good at surprising me, it's my turn to return the favor."

"How did your case go?" They were having small talk. It felt like old times, they were enjoying themselves, alone. With Kalia now being in the forefront, Victor and Yvonne had to steal away time together.

"Good. My client was able to get exactly what she wanted in alimony. I know if we ever divorce, you are going to take me to the cleaners."

"We are not going to divorce." Yvonne said looking him square in the eye. "I got a strange call the other day." The waiter resurfaced. He took away the appetizer plates and replaced them with dinner entrees.

"For the lady," Yvonne's meal consisted of parmesan crumb crusted chicken breast, stuffed with wild mushrooms and lemon herb cream. It was served with fettuccine alfredo and broccoli.

"For you sir," Victor chose for himself Fall off the Bone Ribs smothered in a tangy sweet Hawaiian pineapple sauce. His side dishes were asparagus tips and a baked potato. There was fresh baked bread for the table. The waiter also refreshed their wine for the main course.

"What kind of call?" Victor wanted to continue what his wife started before the waiter came with their entrees.

"Ms. Betsy called with a message from a nurse saying they had test results for Kalia at the hospital." Victor froze. He looked at Yvonne with a blank stare. *This is it*, he thought, *this is going to be the end of my life as I know it.* He knew that his lies would catch up with him one way or another. He was determined that he would almost rather everything hit the fan, than for him to come out with the truth.

"Don't worry," Yvonne responded to the look he had on his face. "I went to the hospital to meet with the doctor yesterday. There was a mistake in the hospital. You are gonna laugh when you hear this, there was a boy named Kalil Russell born on the same day at Crawford Long and he was the baby they were trying to find. I guess because of the same last names or something, you were put down as the father on his file and that's why they called you at the office."

"Oh," Victor said looking at his plate. He stuck his fork into his meat slowly. He was not laughing.

"Baby," Yvonne reached her hand across the table to touch his, "it's okay, Kalia is just fine."

"Wow, when did all this happen?"

"Yesterday."

"Why didn't you tell me about it yesterday?"

"Because, there was no reason to get you all worked up. It was a flub that the hospital was behind."

"I'll go up there…"

"And say what, you want the job of the girl who put your name on the wrong child's file? It was an accident." Victor looked at his wife. Her eyes told the whole story, she knew absolutely nothing. Nor did she suspect anything. She genuinely thought that what happened was a calamity. She saw that his demeanor changed, she presumed that he was upset about what she had just told him.

"Accidents do happen." He knew that he had to regain his composure fast, or she was going to suspect something. He took a bite of his ribs.

"They said it was some kind of genetic disease," Victor almost choked. "I kept trying to put myself in the place of the couple whose child is sick and they don't know. I can't imagine what they are going to go through when they find out that their child has an illness."

"A genetic disease? What kind?"

"I don't remember, some kind of kidney disease." Victor thought back to the call that he got from Monique when she was hysterical saying that Kalil had blood in his diaper. He was finding out from absolutely the most unlikely source that his son had a genetic disease.

"All you do is wish for a healthy child," Victor started on a tirade. "You pray for ten fingers and ten toes. You pray that you child will grow up and be successful, be a good moral person. You never know what may come out of the mix."

"Thank God Kalia is alright. I'm kind of getting nervous though. What if they took that test a long time ago and spelled her name wrong?"

"Didn't the doctor say that it was a boy, Kalil?"

"How did you know his name?" Yvonne eyed her husband suspiciously, her heart was pounding.

"You said it earlier, Baby. Calm down."

"Yes, they said it was a boy," she commented remembering that she had told Victor the boy's name. "But if they can get your name on his file, then who knows what else could be wrong?"

Victor had planned for this night to be all about his wife and their marriage. He wanted them to spend a nice, calming evening just the two of them and made arrangements to do so. The end result was the very disturbing answer to his illegitimate son's illness. He could take this as the opportunity and tell Yvonne the truth now. This would probably be the most perfect prospect at timing that he would ever have.

She knew that Victor's name was on the file. She knew that the boy's name is similar to their daughter's. She knew that he was sick. This would be the time, if any, to tell her that he had an affair on her. Emotionally, she would be so wound up in the outcome, that she would possibly forgive him and focus on the child.

In his mind, Victor was building the perfect scenario. If he told her now, in public, it would force her to react mildly and by the time she could have the response where she could act out, she would be calmed down. He stared across the table at his wife. The ambiance at the restaurant was magical, yet it was not enough to protect him from the realism of his life.

"Yvonne, I need to tell you something." He looked at her directly and wanted to come clean with her. He wanted earnestly to tell her the truth about Monique and Kalil. He knew that Monique would certainly appreciate the honesty. He thought about all he stood to loose in his purge. There was the wife that he absolutely adored. With her went the ability to see his daughter every day. The comfortable and cozy home life that they had built for themselves. Then there was the trust.

Even if Yvonne did forgive him, it would be quite a challenge for him to earn her respect and trust back. There was no way that he could justify having and hiding a 3 year long affair from her. As if that were not bad enough, there was the bombshell about the child. Whenever the news did surface, Victor was going to have to do more than kiss the ground that Yvonne walked on to get her to take him back.

"Ok," Yvonne said twirling the fork in her fettuccine. Her mind was bouncing back and forth between how those innocent parents would feel and getting her own child tested just to be sure.

"I think that we should be grateful for our child's health and celebrate our anniversary." Victor picked up a glass and waited for Yvonne to toast. She smiled. She realized that he was trying to get her mind off of what they were talking about and move on to something that was more lighthearted. The sick child subject put a damper on their celebration.

"I think about when you proposed to me. It was so sweet." Yvonne took the hint and changed the subject. They spoke of only good and positive things during the rest of the meal. Victor had to move on to another subject or he was liable to spill the beans and tell his wife everything. While he knew that was the best thing to do, he still was not ready to deal with the repercussions of his actions.

The desert course came. Yvonne was very excited. She did not know what her husband had ordered, but it looked rather tasty. Her chilled plate bore a double chocolate praline tart with orange sorbet on top. For himself, Victor chose a chocolate swirl cheesecake with whipped cream and Belgian milk chocolate shavings.

Yvonne savored every tasty bite. She wanted the time to last forever. She seemed to be more interested in Victor's desert than her own. He fed her pieces of his and stole pieces of hers. Yvonne was so in love. This was how things used to be, before Kalia, before the sleepless nights and weary days.

Kalia had been the perfect addition to their family. Yvonne hoped that they could maintain the peace that had blessed them for so long before. She felt there was no reason why they could not. Family meant everything to her and Victor and Kalia were her family.

She was clueless as to what else Victor had planned for the night. She did not even care. Yvonne wanted to get her husband home and make sweet love to him. Victor tried to put the news of Kalil in the back of his mind. He knew the glazed over look in his wife's eyes. It was a look he had seen a thousand times.

The waiter came and bought cappuccino for two. It was the last course. He thanked The Russells for their patronage. Yvonne looked around again and saw that the restaurant was thinning out. About only half of the tables were filled. From the booth, they had a view of almost the entire eating area.

"Baby, I just want you to know that you mean the world to me. You and Kalia both are the lights of my life. There is nothing that I won't do for you. I am completely happy in this marriage and no matter what happens..."

"You're scaring me." Yvonne said.

"How?"

"What do you mean no matter what happens?"

"In life, things happen in life. Above all of that, I love you and I always will." He sat there and let it soak in. He was sending a message. He knew now that he could not hide behind his twisted web much longer. The truth was going to come out whether he volunteered the story or someone else did. He hoped that she would reflect on this time, this feeling to pull them through.

"I love you too, Baby. And yes, you have outdone even my best surprise with this early anniversary gift."

"Oh, sweetheart, it gets so much better than this." He kissed her swiftly on the lips, then stood up and asked for her hand. She slid out of the booth and let him escort her out of the restaurant.

"Baby, I really am impressed with this place," she said as they waited for the valet. "We'll have to come here again."

"Yeah, when you start back working," he laughed.

"It's not that expensive," she whispered.

"Is...but that doesn't matter because, you deserve the best." They got into the car and drove down the street a few miles and turned into a hotel.

"Ooh, so it does get better?" Yvonne asked curiously. Of course, there was only so much that could be done at a hotel. She got the hint.

"Ooh yes," he mocked.

"What about my daughter?"

"Rosemary will be watching her until tomorrow."

"Okay." Once again, they pulled into valet. They checked into the hotel and went up to their room. No sooner than Victor cracked open the door, Yvonne smelled the roses. She was thinking how many roses there must be for her to smell them from the outside. Victor was being too slow in opening the door. She pushed him inside.

When he turned on the light, Yvonne gasped. There were rose petals all over the floor. There were 4 boxes on the bed. It was apparent that he had come to set up the room prior to picking her up for dinner. She slid her shoes off and walked on the yellow and red rose petals over to the bed. She looked like a kid in a candy store. She picked up the biggest box and shook it. He laughed at her enthusiasm. She tore into the wrapping.

The first box had Styrofoam bubbles in it. She fished through those until her hands reached something hard. Yvonne wrapped her hands around a box and pulled it out. It was a Lexus RX 300 model, cherry red. It was encased in a Plexiglas case with a wooden bottom. She screamed.

"Baby, I'm getting a new car!!"

"Ah, no I bought you a model sized version." He squashed her dream using a smart alec voice.

"You're joking me right?"

"No. I told you, now is not the time to buy a new car. So I bought you the next best thing." Yvonne looked at him, like he was playing around with her. There were 3 other boxes on the bed. She was sure that at least one of the other boxes had a set of keys or an electronic keychain.

She jumped into the second largest box. It was filled with tissue paper. Yvonne pulled the tissue paper out. The suspense was building. At the bottom of the box, she found a whoopi cushion.

"Baby, are all of these prank gifts?" She asked clearly aggravated.

"No," he stood with his back up against the dresser. With that smirk on his face, she did not believe him.

"I'm done, I'm going to sleep." Yvonne undid her belt and laid down on the bed.

"Baby, be a good sport."

"You mean be entertainment for you?"

"Open up another box," he begged. Yvonne sat up, looked at him and then looked at the two unopened boxes. She painstakingly unwrapped the paper on the smallest box. She was sure that it was another gag gift. So when she got down to the box, she opened it and made a funny face.

"Ooh, I love it," she said blandly without looking into the box.

"Look in the box Yvonne," her husband urged. She found a beautiful "O" pendant. It was a yellow gold necklace with a charm that was a diamond encrusted "O".

"I love it! Its just the right size!" She jumped up and pushed her husband out of the way so she could see in the mirror. He took the necklace from her and he clasped it around her neck.

She kissed him lightly on the cheek and then flew back over to the bed. She crossed her fingers that there were keys to a new Lexus in the only remaining box. As she opened it, she bounced up and down on the bed, humming like a small child. He could see that she was excited. In the smallest box she found a folded up note that said, *Go to the bathroom.*

"Oh so now we're playing scavenger hunt." She said prying herself off of the bed. She made her way to the bathroom and he heard her start to giggle. Then the door closed. A few moments later, she emerged out of the bathroom. She was wearing a sexy number. It was a turquoise two piece, bra and panty with black filigree accents. Her legs were covered with thigh high lace stockings and a pair of black high heel shoes. Victor had the biggest smile on his face.

"Is this what you've wanted to see me in all night big boy?" She asked him in a low, seductive tone.

"Umm hmm," he said shaking his head.

"Here it is," she stepped back with her arms widespread and let him view the present he bought for her. She turned around so that he could see just how good she looked. Yvonne took her hair out of a ponytail and it was hanging free with a huge curl hanging just to the side of her eye.

"Awesome," he murmured.

"That's it? All I get is awesome?" She stepped back over to him, this time between his legs. He already knew what time it was. She knelt down and unbuttoned his pants and pulled his manhood through his boxers. She took him into her mouth. Victor leaned his head back and allowed himself to be pleasured. Just when she could tell that it was really getting good to him, she stopped and stood up.

"Lay on the bed," she ordered him. He quickly obeyed her command. Victor stretched himself out on the bed and allowed himself to be teased. She straddled him and rocked gently. Yvonne bent down to kiss him. Hungrily, he met her mouth and held on to her. They kissed each other with a passion and fire like when they first made real, true love. He ran his fingers down her back and unclasped the bra. He carefully pulled it down and Yvonne took her arms out of it.

He rolled over and got on top of her. They stopped kissing, he drew back and took her panties off, then stared at her while he removed his shirt. She sat up wrapped her hands around his neck and brought him back down to her. She rolled back over on top of him and mounted him, this time, she meant business.

Victor found his way inside of her and she rocked and rocked. She knew that he liked when she was in control. She liked being in control. He placed his hands on her waist and helped her gyrate. They were both moaning and panting. She was rubbing her hands up and down his chest.

They were stimulating each other. The intensity increased and Victor laid back and started to exhale loudly. Yvonne, herself, could feel the satisfaction that she was giving her husband. All of a sudden, she stopped moving and stood up on the bed. She turned around to face his feet and Victor opened his eyes to appreciate the view. Her thigh high lace stockings were all that she had on. She sat on his lap, using her feet to push off.

She was driving him crazy. He propped himself up to watch her in the mirror. Being able to see views of her from the front and the back instantly brought him to a climax. Yvonne helped maintain the tingling sensation by running her hands up and down his lower abdomen and thighs. They both lay sprawled out, catching their breath. It was an unforgettable anniversary.

Victor knew that it was going to be hard for him to get away to call Monique to tell her what Yvonne had found out. It did not help that it was the weekend and the branch of the hospital where Dr. Anderson's office was, only took appointments during the week. He played it safe and decided to wait until Monday to tell her. That way, he could be free to go to the hospital with her.

Throughout the course of the weekend, Yvonne kept bringing up the subject that she was still very concerned about her daughter's health. Victor and Rosemary tried to convince her that she had nothing to worry about. She was not convinced.

"Yvonne, you do not need to have Kalia tested for anything."

"How do you know that? I told you before that they could have mixed up the test results or they could be from a long time ago."

"There is nothing to worry about."

"Why not?"

"Trust me!" Victor was loosing his temper with the whole thing.

"How do you know? Do you know that she is totally healthy? Do you? Do you?" Yvonne was getting visibly perturbed.

"Trust me!"

"Why should I trust you? You keep telling me to trust you but you're not giving me any reason to." Victor knew that depending on the way he answered that question he could jeopardize his life and entire future.

"I just think that you should not get yourself all worked up." It was not often that they yelled at each other or even raised their voices. This questionable situation was bringing that out of them both.

"Is there any harm in me going to get a test done just to be sure? That's why we pay for insurance."

"If you want to get it done, do it yourself."

"Do it myself? So what you are saying is that you don't care anything about her well being."

"I do, I just don't want to add any fuel to the fire."

"Thanks Victor, it's nice to know that I have your full support!" She said sarcastically. Yvonne stormed out of the back door and sat on the back porch to get some fresh air. The fence they put up gave her peace. She needed time to decide whether or not she was blowing this out of proportion or if she was using her head.

Chapter 10

Monday morning came. No sooner than he backed out of the driveway, he called Monique. He told her that he was on his way and that she needed to call in to work. He tried not to sound urgent and told her that they should go to the hospital since they had not heard anything from the tests. Victor could not tell her the truth being that far away. He knew how she was going to take it.

He arrived at her house earlier than most people even left for work. Monique was eager to see him and happy that he was taking the stance that he was even if he had to sneak around to do it. She met him at the door. His stomach was turning and he felt sick. He was going to have to look this woman in the eye and tell her that their child had a genetic disease that he had no other clues about. Victor hated to be the bearer of bad news.

"Good morning." They greeted each other at the same time.

"Where did all this come from?" Monique asked about him going out of his way to stop by on his way to work and on a Monday no less.

"We need to talk."

"About you not wanting to wait for the results to come back? I think that's cool. Being here with Kalil all weekend has pretty much put me in the same mind frame."

"No, have a seat." Monique recollected the last time he told her to have a seat in that tone. She did not want to then, but thought this time, she would heed to the warning.

"I'm sitting," she said after finding a place on the couch and Victor took too long to speak. He was wringing his hands together. Monique was very nervous.

"Yvonne told me that she got a call…"

"Victor, I did not call her," she spoke up defensively.

"I know that. She got a call from the hospital. It seems that some kind of way they called my job to talk to me. I was in court all day so Ms. Betsy, being concerned, called Yvonne and gave her the nurse's message." Monique put her hands over her mouth. Victor could see that she seemed to be in shock.

"Oh no," she whispered trying to stifle her jubilation of Yvonne recently finding out.

"Yeah, she went in to tell them that there was a mistake and somehow, the doctor told her what was wrong with Kalil. Not the entire answer, but at least we have a start."

"What?"

"He has a genetic kidney disorder or disease."

"Genetic?" Monique sat back on the couch and closed her eyes. She let out a loud breath and tried to let it soak in. How could her infant son have a genetic disease?

"That's all I know."

"We have to get him to the hospital now." Monique stood up and walked into the room where Kalil was.

"I'll fix his bag, you get him dressed. We can be out of here in a minute." Victor was taking charge and wanted to get things done in a timely manner. In less than 10 minutes, they were on their way out the door.

Victor called Ms. Betsy and left a message saying that he forgot to write a court date on the calendar and that he would be out of the office all day. He had to call her before she got there, otherwise, it would have been a big production. She would have asked questions, prying. This way, he got the point across and turned his phone off. All of his attention was now on his ailing son.

They arrived at the hospital office downtown Atlanta, amid morning rush hour traffic. Going through every foot of traffic was worth it. It put them that much closer to getting where they had to go. All hell was breaking loose on I-75 headed towards downtown. There was not much talking going on inside the car. They were both in their own worlds and rightfully so. Neither one of them knew what else to expect. The information could have a palpable healing process or there could be no cure.

Monique stared out the window. Although she cared about the outcome, it made her feel better that the father of her child was there with her this time. She turned around to look at her little prince. He seemed to be doing fine. He wiggled around when he saw his mother looking at him. His face beamed at her. His smile made her smile. It was so blameless. Kalil did not know what all the fuss was about and could care less.

Victor glanced at Kalil in the rearview mirror. He was very worried about the boy's health. He had to be, it was his son. He would rather be no other place in the world than with his son when the whole answer came out. He took his hand and placed it on Monique's lap. She turned around to face the front again. She looked at him and put her hand on top of his.

They arrived at the doctor's office just before 8. The office did not open until 8:30. They found some chairs in the main lobby and decided to just wait it out. The air between them was so dense. The lack of conversation had nothing to do with anger or hatred and everything to do with nervousness.

Victor was holding Kalil in his lap. His foot was anxiously bouncing up and down. Monique was pacing back and forth. Her arms were folded across her chest. She could hear the sounds of the clock ticking overhead. Not knowing was eating her alive.

After what seemed like an eternity, the time had come for them to go upstairs to the office. Monique told the receptionist who they were and that they needed to see Dr. Anderson.

"You are Kalil Russell's mother?" The receptionist asked.

"Yes," Monique replied irritated. The young receptionist could sense the urgency and excused herself to tell Dr. Anderson. He came back around with her.

"Dr. Anderson," he stuck out his hand.

"Monique Crenshaw and this is Victor Russell."

"Victor Russell?"

"Yes," Victor knew exactly why the doctor asked that. His wife claimed the office called his job who then alerted his wife. It was also her who told the doctor that it was all a paperwork mix-up.

"Let's go to my office, shall we?" Dr. Anderson led, followed by Monique, then Victor and Kalil.

"Dr. Anderson," Victor piped up, "could you please tell us what is going on with our son."

"Kalil has a rare genetic kidney disease called polycystic kidney disease, PKD."

"Oh," a whimper escaped Monique's mouth. The build up had been too much. At least Dr. Anderson skipped the preamble. Once he put two and two together about

Victor, he decided against any further needless conversation.

"We detected this with the ultrasound. The attending physician who did the initial tests was very thorough since I could not get right to you. There are 4 cysts in his left kidney and 1 in the other. It says on Kalil's chart that you saw blood in his urine."

"Yes I did."

"Is it getting any worse?"

"Not necessarily, about every other diaper." She answered weakly. "The urination is very frequent, though."

"Hematuria, which is blood in the urine and cysts in the kidney are indicative of PKD. Since the cysts are still a part of the kidney, the disease is still in its beginning stages. He presents another symptom, elevated blood pressure. As the disease progresses, the cysts eventually separate from the kidneys and continue to enlarge."

"This disease occurs two ways," he continued. "The main way is that it is inherited where the symptoms occur between 30 and 40 years of age. 90 per cent of PKD cases are that, autosomal dominant PKD. The other is autosomal recessive PKD which can begin as early as the womb. Do either of you have PKD or carry the gene for it?"

"My father died of kidney failure when I was younger." Monique offered.

"I don't know anything about my parents. I'm an orphan."

"In the case of autosomal recessive PKD, both parents must be carriers of the disease. Since Victor does not know his parental background and Monique's father died of kidney failure, it's very possible."

"What are the other symptoms?" Victor earnestly wanted to know.

"Let's see," Dr. Anderson fiddled around with the papers on his desk. "Urinary tract infection, hemorrhoids, varicose veins, low blood-cell count and end stage renal disease." Dr. Anderson looked up at them. They both had the feigned indifference of being run over by a tractor trailer. The news was clearly hitting them hard.

"End stage renal disease?" Victor repeated.

"This can't be happening," Monique said and tears started rolling down her face.

"What can be done about all this?" Victor was trying to be level headed.

"Kalil can be given antibiotics to control urinary tract infections and medicine for high blood pressure. His diet is going to have to be nutritious. In the event of kidney failure, he will have to receive dialysis or a transplant."

"Dialysis? A transplant? Dr. Anderson are you saying that there is no cure for this?" Monique cried.

"There is no cure," he said humbly. "But transplants among end stage renal disease patients have been tremendously successful. The healthy kidneys do not develop cysts." Monique turned her attention to Victor. He knew precisely what was on her mind. She was thinking about his other child. That was no secret in Dr. Anderson's office. They all knew the truth.

"Give me my baby." Monique took Kalil from Victor's loving hold. "Dr. Anderson, are you saying that we have to wait on some poor baby to die in order for my Kalil to live?"

"No," he answered curiously, "we can test another child to be a donor. More often than not, end renal stage disease occurs mostly in adults like I said earlier. You both know that we all are born with 2 kidneys. Usually, a loved one will donate a kidney so that the ill person may live."

"So, what about siblings?" Monique asked dryly. It was almost vindictive the tone that she used. From what Dr. Anderson could figure out, Victor was married to another woman, who also had his child. Monique was someone on the side. What he did not know was whether or not Victor and Monique had a preexisting relationship. Monique seemed scorned, even though she was sitting in the doctor's office with Victor. It appeared that they were together first, then Victor went and married someone else and Monique came back into the picture.

Whatever the situation, Monique was no holds barred, even in front of Dr. Anderson. To him, that said Monique did not care who knew what about her life and what was going on. Her mind was set on helping her child. That was it.

"Siblings who share both parents are not good matches. They can both have the disease or the trait for it."

"Ultimately, what are our choices?" Victor asked.

"We can wait to see what happens, in due course though, it will come down to transplantation or death." Monique buried her face in the crook of Kalil's neck. She was trying to hold in her sobs, but was a bit unsuccessful.

Dr. Anderson handed her a few tissues and Victor took Kalil back. Then Kalil began to whine. The doctor had been in this place time and time again. He had to tell parents that their child was sick and would not get better be it by birth, an accident or simply by design. Dr. Anderson never had children for that reason. He could not imagine what it must be like on the other side of that desk.

Feeling that it was his obligation, Victor slid his chair closer to Monique to comfort her. He put his arm around her and Dr. Anderson excused himself for a minute. He had to regroup. This situation was going to be more complicated than normal. The father was clearly in the middle. He was going to have to choose whose life he thought was more important. One way or another, some young lady's heart was going to be ripped out.

"I don't understand," Monique said shaking her head.

"It's the nature of the beast."

"Don't you sit there and tell me about the nature of the damn beast!" Her whisper was angry.

"Some things we can't change."

"Some things we can. I love my son and I don't want to see him die without ever having a chance. Now, you know what you have to do. Don't be a coward. Stand up and be a man!" She stood up and adjusted her clothes.

"You're ready to go?" Victor questioned her.

"There's nothing else to do here. You need to come up with a plan to save my son's life." Dr. Anderson walked back in.

"Dr. Anderson, do you have a card?" Victor spoke standing up next to Monique.

"Here's one for both of you. If you have any further questions, feel free to call." He escorted them to the door and gave a closing salutation.

"That took a long time," the receptionist commented.

"Its going to take even longer. That guy has a major predicament on his hands. His wife is so much prettier." The last comment was made as an aside.

On the other side of town, Yvonne was on the floor in the living room playing with Kalia. Kalia was squealing and clapping her hands. The T.V. was on, but it only had her partial attention. Kalia was crawling around and scooting. Yvonne had a ball watching her explore. For now, anyway, her exploration was pretty harmless. She was not old enough to pull up or really play with knobs. Yvonne could restrict her movement to whatever area she wanted. There was a knock on the door. Yvonne grabbed Kalia and walked to the door.

"I have a delivery for Yvonne Russell," the man said.

"A delivery?" Yvonne looked at him like he was crazy. She did not see anything in his hands.

"Yes, over here," he pointed towards the yard. Yvonne stepped out of the house to see around it. There sat a cherry red Lexus RX300. She screamed and gave Kalia to the man at her door. He grasped the happy baby using fast reflexes to keep her from falling. She looked at the street and saw another gentleman in a Lexus waving at her. She figured they were a delivery service.

"Whoa! Woo-hoo!" Yvonne yelled at the top of her lungs. She ran over to her new vehicle. It had a huge red bow on top of it. She walked around it, taking it all in and running her hands around it just barely touching. When she got back around to the driver side she opened the door and sat down.

Yvonne took a deep breath to take in the new car smell. She put her hands on the wooden steering wheel and leaned back in the seat. She could not believe that her husband managed to surprise her again. Rosemary heard all the noise and came running outside.

"Oh my goodness!" She walked across the lawn barefoot to take a look at the new car.

"Its for our anniversary!" Yvonne hopped out and she and Rosemary gleefully hugged each other.

"Alright, now move outta my way. I want to see this new wagon." Rosemary joked.

"My, my, my. A baby and a new car in just a few months," Susan said walking up. "I'm very impressed with you Mrs. Russell. You are certainly becoming accustomed to this New Mommy Club living." She gave Yvonne a high five.

"Mrs. Russell, all I need is a signature from you."

"Oh, I'm sorry." Yvonne met with the gentleman, signed the form and retrieved her baby bundle. The gentleman handed over the keys, excused himself and let the ladies get on with the celebration.

"I am so amazed! Yes!" Yvonne was clearly excited about her new vehicle. After they all systematically examined the new vehicle, Rosemary had a bright idea.

"Let's take a ride in the new truck!"

"How are we going to do that with 3 three kids who all need to be in car seats?" Susan was thinking logically.

"We can put Jackson in the back. All long as he has a blanket, he'll lay back there all day." Rosemary said.

"No, we can't do that." Yvonne argued.

"Jackson, you want to ride in the back so you can look up at the sky through the big window? You can name the clouds, but you have to lie on your back."

"Yeah!" Jackson yelled and did a little dance. "I wanna see clouds!" He ran to the back of the truck and stood there waiting on someone to let him in the truck.

"Alright, alright, since our New Mommies Club meeting is cancelled this week, we can go have brunch," Yvonne suggested.

"Let's go clean up and meet back here in 10 minutes," Rosemary said. All of the ladies agreed. The first thing Yvonne did was go pick up the phone. She had a fleeting thought about driving down to his job, but Rosemary changed that plan for her. She called Bowles and Laughton and of course, none other than Ms. Betsy answered the call. She told Yvonne that Victor was in court, it was a last minute detail.

Yvonne was really disappointed. She wanted to talk to him right away. She figured that she would call his phone periodically to try and catch him at lunch. He had done so well at not slipping up and telling her. She could not believe that he kept that hidden from her for so long. Usually, he would drop a hint like, 'Wait til you see what I got you,' or something to that effect.

Susan and Rosemary were standing in the driveway ten minutes later and Yvonne was yelling out at them that she would be outside in a minute. Rosemary went and got the keys from her so they could start loading up. Shortly there after, they were on their way to lunch.

"So tell us Yvonne, how did you manage to get this?" Susan started.

"I told you its for our anniversary," she said through laughs. Her story was not compelling.

"Right, your anniversary is not for another couple of weeks." Susan noted.

"She's right. On Friday, Victor asked me to watch Kalia, he took Yvonne out on a pre-anniversary date. He said that she would never expect it." Rosemary volunteered.

"Must be nice," Susan said looking all around the interior.

"I am so happy," Yvonne said.

"I'd be happy if I got a new car that I was not paying for too!"

"No, I mean I am so happy with my marriage, with my family. I thought everything would be awkward now with Kalia." She heard her name and looked up at her mother. "But it's not at all. We still sit down and talk, I've had to find a way to cook meals faster though."

"Tell me about it," Rosemary laughed.

"I mean really, I think at this point in our relationship, it feels like we have reached a whole new plateau."

"Good, honey," Susan scoffed, "now you focus on driving. I'm hungry." They all laughed as Yvonne chauffeured them to their destination. She was feeling so good that lunch was on her.

Victor saw the old, faded Sparky's sign and knew that he had made it to heaven. At this point, which was the lowest in his life, this was as good as it got. He was backed into a corner. He built the walls mainly by himself, with a little help from Monique. If it were not for her, then the relationship would have ended a long time ago. They had stopped having sex more than a year prior, but that's when the situation took a turn for the worse. Now, the child that came from his affair was deathly ill and there was no way that he could go on without telling Yvonne. There would be endless doctor's visits, consultations, tests and even possibly surgeries.

If he could not be there for all of them, then he would have to do his best. He drug his feet one before the other until he reached the inside. He walked over to the bar and told Sonya that he would be in a booth in the rear of the joint and to bring him 5 shots.

She had a feeling that it had all hit the fan. She had no idea what he was about to tell her. Sonya, being a woman herself, knew all the ways that Yvonne could have taken the situation. Little did Sonya know, Yvonne had no clue yet, Victor was simply dreading the inevitable. Sonya did not say anything. She slid the serving tray on the table in front of him, then sat down across from him. She told the other bartenders that she was taking a break.

Victor picked up the first drink, nodded his head at Sonya, then gulped it down. He wiped his mouth with the back of his hand and slammed the glass down. The second shot, came in much the same fashion. The third shot, he winked at Sonya, then downed it. He looked up towards the ceiling and exhaled, then polished off the fourth shot. Sonya was looking in amazement. She had never seen him drink that many shots in a row, she knew the story had to be a bad one.

"You know Sonya, I've really, really, really done it this time. I don't think my life will ever be the same. I have to go home and tell the woman that I love, I cheated on her for 3 years." Sonya looked at him confused.

"What do you mean? You still didn't tell Yvonne about anything?"

"Not yet, but I'm gonna have to."

"What happened that was so serious that its forcing you to have to tell her? Did Monique give you a final ultimatum?" She did not understand why he was going through all these motions and Yvonne still had no knowledge of his infidelity. More so than that, why did he all of a sudden now, have to tell her?

"No, we haven't been intimate in about a year now. It's Kalil."

"What? Victor, you aren't saying anything," she probed.

"Kalil is sick. He has a genetic disease and he's going to need some long term medical attention."

"What kind of disease?" Her heart was slowly sinking.

"Kidney, in the end, the doctor said it's transplantation or sure death. He could be put on dialysis, but that would only last so long."

"I'm so sorry, Victor. I am truly sorry. My heart goes out to you." As she said the words, he put his head down on the table. She looked at him for the pitiful sight that he was. Now was certainly not the time for an 'I told you so'. The situation could have been nipped in the bud a long time ago. He chose to let it carry on.

The words that she spoke were sincere. Sonya would have done anything in her power to take him out of that circumstance. But it was in the hands of a greater power. He had gotten himself into it and now he had to get himself out.

"Because the illness has no cure, he's going to be in and out of the hospitals probably for his entire life if we can't find a donor. I can't expect Monique to go through all that by herself. She is going to need someone to depend on. I am his father."

"That's the problem. You have to tell your wife that you are going to support another woman. That will be tough," her honesty was brutal.

"I know, man, Yvonne is..." he sat up and took the last shot.

"You look like you want to cry."

"I do," his response was weak. She got up from her side of the booth and sat down next to him.

"I know right now, you can't see the end in sight. In due time, it will get better."

"Hmm," he replied just to let her know he was listening.

"You are not a bad person, Victor. You just make bad decisions. You don't really think things through. You don't think about the people that will suffer as a result of your actions."

"I just didn't think that it would ever get this far. It was just sex."

"It was just sex but it was sex with a woman who wanted to be in your woman's place. It was sex with a co-worker that could have cost you both your jobs. If it was just sex, you should have left it at that. There should have been no gift exchange or talking to her about your marriage. Hell, at the point when you got married, you should have cut her off completely."

"I appreciate that, but none of that is going to help me now."

"It will in the long run. From now on, you will really consider what you are doing and who you are doing it to."

"I need another shot."

"The bar's clean." That was Sonya's way of telling him that drinks were off limits to him.

"C'mon, Sonya." He urged angrily.

"Boy, you must be foolin'. You have to drive yourself home. If I didn't know any better, I would be offering you a cab. But I know that you will sit here and regain your composure before you leave."

"I can't face her sober, I can't."

"I'll go get you a bottle of water and some wings," Sonya got up from the booth. By the time she put in the food order and grabbed a bottle of water from the cooler, she looked up and Victor was gone.

Victor thought about all of the times that he had taken the trip home leaving from Monique's house. The guilt was consuming him. He wished like hell that it would have consumed him then. He and Yvonne were about to celebrate their 3 year anniversary. Three years and he had not held to their vows in the least. Well, he did not put any other before her, unless having sex before leaving the office counted. To him, the fourth year did not count since they stopped having sex.

Driving down their street, he saw his anniversary gift to her. It was beautiful, just what she wanted. *Damn*, he thought to himself. He pulled into the driveway. Victor couldn't get out of the car soon enough, he threw up just outside of the car door.

"I'm glad you got it in the grass," Yvonne said holding Kalia. She heard him drive up, just as he knew she would. He was doubled over and waved her to stay where she was. He did not want her coming over to comfort him. He stood there for a while to make sure that he got it all out. The funny part was that his throwing up had nothing to do with the drinking and everything to do with what he was about to do.

"Thank you for my truck, Baby!" Yvonne said excitedly when he finally came in. "I know it's the last thing you want to hear right now, but I've been waiting hours to get that off my chest. What's wrong with you?"

"I'm stressed."

"Stressed about what?" Victor made his way into the downstairs bathroom to rinse his mouth out.

"Life."

"Victor, what are you talking about?" She looked at him strangely. Yvonne put Kalia in the baby pen and turned her attention to her husband.

"Yvonne, I've made some mistakes."

"Ok," she listened intently scared of what he was about to say.

"These mistakes could very well cost me my family."

"But me and Kalia are your..." She started on the defensive then she realized what he was saying.

"I know Baby, I know." He walked over to her and grabbed her hands, sitting her down on the couch. Kalia was watching T.V., she could have cared less what was going on behind her.

"I had an affair," he paused to pick his words carefully. "It started at work. Remember when I...Okay what happened was...Did you ever see..."

"Victor, calm down, you are talking crazy. You stopped by Sparky's today didn't you?"

"Yeah."

"Let's get you to bed," she stood up and reached for his hand.

"Let's talk," he pulled her down.

"Baby, I..." he put his finger over her mouth.

"I had an affair with a para at my job, Monique. We started sleeping together before you and I got engaged. To make a long story short, I only just stopped sleeping with her when she told me that she was pregnant a little over a year ago."

"What?...You got a girl pregnant?"

"We stopped sleeping together a year ago," Yvonne could feel her temperature rising. Her body was getting hot. "She knew about you and she knows about Kalia."

"So, if ya'll aren't sleeping together anymore then..."

"When she told me she was pregnant, I told her in no way I going to risk loosing my family for her. I never sold her any dreams, she knew where my heart was. The agreement was to have an abortion. She reneged on the deal. She said something about being too far along. The child that she had was a boy." Yvonne sat there in complete shock. She could not process what she was hearing. This could not be true.

"His name was Kalil."

"Oh," she exclaimed. It just slipped out. That was the glue. Her hands found themselves covering her face. She knew where this was going. The story now had a meaning.

"The call that you got was not a wrong number and the hospital did not mess anything up. Kalil Russell is my son."

"How could you!" She screamed, "how could you do that to us?" Kalia's head snapped back to hear what startled her.

"Yvonne, I'm sorry. There's no excuse."

"You're damned right there's no excuse. I do everything for you Victor!"

"There's more."

"What?"

"There's more I have to tell you."

"How could there be more?"

"Kalil is sick." As soon as the words escaped his lips, she remembered Dr. Anderson.

"Oh my goodness," she said in an undertone.

"The kidney disease that you haphazardly found out about has no cure. The only solution is transplantation. Other than that, the alternative is death. Today, I was not in court, I was at the hospital finding out what we could to about the illness."

"We?"

"Me and Monique." Yvonne put her hands on her abdomen. She was sick to her stomach. Though the child was not hers, she had been imaging how the parents must feel and now she was close enough to the issue to feel the pain. Then she thought about the pregnant paralegal at the office story that Victor lied about.

She needed to have time to process what her husband had just said to her. First he said that he had been having an affair. Then he said that he got married to her while maintaining his affair. That was followed by saying there was an illegitimate pregnancy that he tried to end, which validated his wrongdoings. The pregnancy was never terminated leading instead to a child with a deadly disease.

Victor did not want to look at her. She was leaned back on the throw pillows of their plush couch. The couch where they had made love countless number of times. He could not see her face and preferred to keep it that way. He maintained looking downward knowing that he would loose it if he saw her cry.

Her response was scaring him. She was not moving, he could not hear her sniffling which signified that she probably was not crying. She was not breathing heavily, nor jumping up and down screaming. She was calm. Too calm.

Yvonne looked at her child. She was so innocent in all of this, they both were. Victor had taken it upon himself to go out and ruin everything. Yvonne looked around at her home and thought that everything, the house, the love, the vows, the family was all built on lies.

"Kalil Russell is your child." She said it more as a statement than a question.

"Yes."

"I thought that it seemed like too big of a coincidence. I just kept telling myself that it was all a mistake. It was the hospital's fault. Not in my wildest dreams did I want to think that...you...were actually his father." Her words were slow and deliberate.

Yvonne exhaled and stood up from the couch. She walked outside and drove off in her new truck.

Chapter 11

Yvonne had never felt so sick in all her life. She sensed her whole life was being turned upside down. The man whom she had dedicated her entire existence to had deceived her. The whole reason that she left her old life in the projects was to start anew and create an existence of people who she could trust. There were 2 constants in her life, Victor and Mary Louise.

She could never see him the same way. There was no reason for Victor to have treated her the way that he had. She did not pressure him to get married. That was mostly his idea. And for what? The whole time that they were together, he was seeking pleasure from an outside source.

There was more to it than pleasure. He had ultimately shared himself, which meant more to Yvonne than just sex. He obviously cared for Monique or else the affair would not have lasted as long as it had. She could not take anything he said to heart. The whole speech he gave her about not selling Monique any dreams, could have been more lies. How was Yvonne to know that her husband had no plans to leave her alone with a child?

The street lights were on, but Yvonne had driven down the road so many times that she could do so with her eyes closed. With the darkness settling in, she knew that aimlessly wandering the streets was not something in her best interest to do. She needed to figure a place to go and get her head together. Her first thought was Mary Louise's house. That would be the first place that her husband looked. For the most part she was without friends and family. She finally decided that a hotel would have to do.

She drove past 10 places where she could have laid her head, but they were all in Fayette County. Getting out of the city limits was not enough, she needed to get farther away. As Yvonne put more miles between herself and her home, the burden of her now reality got heavier and heavier. Her cell phone rang. Steering with one hand, she fumbled through her purse to silence the ringer. She was 99.9% sure that it was Victor. She turned her phone off.

Finally, she got tired of driving and felt that 30 minutes was far enough from the world she once knew as familiar. She checked into a hotel, alone and with no belongings other than her purse and a pair of shades. When she got to her room, the first thing she did was get the ice bucket and fill it from the machine down the hall. She purchased a bottled water and headed back to the room. She pulled her hair into a loose bun and stretched out across the bed.

Yvonne had no idea what direction she was supposed to go. Her whole life as she knew it had turned out to be a lie. Curled up in the fetal position, she tried to get her mind together. Certainly, she could find a solution to the problem. Holding strong to the values that Mary Louise had instilled in her over the years, she knew that she had options. Options that she would have preferred never to have had to deal with.

Victor had definitely pulled the wool over her eyes. Lying there on the bed, in a hotel, in the dark, she felt alone. Thoughts were spilling out of her mind and littered the room with the stench. Her husband had cheated on her for years. She did not know whether or not she would be able to ever go back to the life that she once knew. She finally broke down.

She grabbed a pillow and folded it under her head. She had to protect her daughter, no matter what. Victor, working for a law firm, specializing in divorce law, was going to try to take her for all that he could. He did not want to support her, should they end up in divorce court. Kalia had to be taken care of. It was not her fault that her father could not hold to his promises.

The enormity of Victor's other family was really hitting home. It was not a situation that they could just hold hands and walk away from. This other child had an incurable illness. The point being, if she decided to stay, she would have to deal with this child and his mother. She would need to be able to hold her head up high and support Victor in his endeavors. Yvonne was not sure whether or not she could muster the strength for that kind of life.

Rain started to pound on her window. It was as if the heavens understood what she was going through. Lightning illuminated the room through spaces around the curtain. She lugged herself off of the bed and walked over to the sliding glass balcony door. She had to conjure up the muscle to open it, then she stepped out. Her feet gently touching the wet cement and the rain drops falling on her.

It was incredible, the feeling that she got from letting nature bathe her. The trickle of the water seemed to massage her. She tilted her face towards the sky and took in a deep cleansing breath. Exhaling slowly while counting to ten, Yvonne felt her wall come crashing down. She sat on the chair and broke down completely. For the first time she felt that it was alright to cry.

There was no one around to see her or hear her. The only sound that she heard was the sound of the rain, beating down heavily on all the concrete around her. If anyone did happen to see or hear her, she did not care. She was totally absolved in the circumstance of her situation. The sobs that she tried so hard to contain in front of Victor were overwhelming. She was having a cry like her husband had died.

To her, he may as well have. Everything he told her was lie, she felt. Everything he stood for, was a lie. He may as well have left the house one morning and never come back. She had done nothing to deserve what he had done to her. She sat there and cried. Her heart was aching, her soul was confused, her mind was blown.

Under the same rainy sky, Victor was holding on to their daughter, Kalia. She had fallen asleep, feeling protected in his arms. He looked down at her and thought about how he had let her mother down. He thought about what this was going to do to their family. He wondered if his wife were ever coming home.

He had no earthly idea where Yvonne had driven off to. She just walked away from the couch, grabbed her purse and walked out of the door. He had not seen or heard from her since. He tried calling her cell phone, but after 20 some odd calls, he realized she was not going to power back on her phone. Her voicemail held one lone message from him. In it, he did the only thing he could do, apologize.

He had to know that sooner or later this day would come. Especially with Monique so eager to take Yvonne's place. He kept putting it off and putting it off. He cursed himself for getting caught. He should have taken her to the clinic himself instead of leaving her to go do something that she did not want to do on her own. The T.V. was off, so were all of the lights in the house except the kitchen light, which illuminated the living room where they were.

Now, all of a sudden, he was forced to imagine life without Yvonne. He was sitting there not knowing if and when she would put her key in the door. Knowing that if he went to bed, it would be cold and he would be there alone. The reality that she could very well come back and things not be the same was shaking him like a seizure. The fact that his wife's first reaction to the news was to leave, was a clue that she may not stick around.

The thunder roared through the house. He heard a mild tremble inside of things vibrating. He rubbed his eyes and kept them fixed on the front door. His focus, in the dark, was a shiny hint of the doorknob. He prayed that his wife would come back.

The lightning was bringing about a new chapter for Monique. She had been handling the news of her son's illness. It meant that now, Victor would have to bring his secrets to the light. Monique was facing a twofold answer. Either his wife would stay and help Victor through Kalil's illness, or she would leave him and he would cling to Monique. She hoped for the latter.

No matter which outcome, she knew that at the least, he was going to be there for her to help deal with the disease. Having a more intimate knowledge of what was in front of her, the future looked very bleak. She was in love with a little boy who they were telling her may die long before he was able to fulfill her dreams of growing up. Fate had damned him before he even had a chance. She reflected on her conversation with her roommate's reaction to Kalil's illness.

"Girl, you're kidding! Oh no," Alicia exclaimed putting her hand over her heart.

"Yeah, Victor came with me to the hospital this morning."

"What did he have to say?"

"What do you mean? What could he say? We are both upset about it, but it's out of our control."

"You ain't lying." Alicia was sitting there in shock of what her friend was telling her.

"I had been fighting with Victor to tell his wife about us."

"About us who?"

"Me and Kalil."

"She still doesn't know about you and Victor after all this time?"

"No and it's been a constant issue with us for the longest."

"Most men don't just own up to their affairs."

"But there is a child involved here. He needs to take care of his responsibilities."

"The last time I checked, my fridge was packed," Alicia said. She knew what her friend was up to. The girl had been trying to break up Victor and Yvonne from day one.

"Yeah, but he can't deny his child to anyone. What kind of man is that? Anyway, back to what I was saying. I almost feel like Kalil being sick is my fault."

"Because you think it comes from your side?"

"No because I think this all stems from my selfishness. I want Victor to myself and I thought that having this baby would give me a chance." Her words were honest and her voice was somber.

"Nique, you didn't really believe that you having a baby would change his mind about you?" Alicia aimed at Monique.

"I thought that," Monique exhaled, "it would bring us closer."

"That is the dumbest thing I have ever heard."

"Alicia, you use people too."

"It would be using Victor if the doctor told you that you were going to have to have a hysterectomy and you needed to have a child immediately. That, is using. You were being just plain dumb. Nique, I told you a long time ago not to get further involved with that man. Your only defense was how his wife wasn't doing her job."

"I guess I should have listened."

"Damn right you should have listened. Now you are going through so much unnecessary agony. Both you and him, not to mention the innocents, Yvonne and the kids. All of this and you're still no closer to your goal of having him all to yourself."

"Do you think he hates me?"

"If anything, I think he's more upset at himself for letting it get this far. Secondly, yes he's pissed with you for having Kalil. Whose bright idea was it to name the kids Kalia and Kalil?" Alicia asked. Monique told how that was Victor's response to naming the child after him.

"I kind of feel all of this is like karma. The reason my son is sick is because of what I did. I was trying to break up Yvonne's home." Monique was clearly disturbed. Alicia could see that she was straight forward.

"Karma is nothing to play with. What goes around, comes around."

"Why did it have to take my son?" Monique's heart was breaking.

"He's not gone, Nique. He's sick and the doctor did say that there was something that could be done. You're already giving up before you even try." Alicia tried to offer some solace.

"I just feel so bad," Monique could feel the tears welling up in her eyes.

"I wouldn't be your friend if I told you that you shouldn't feel bad. Of course, you never knew that this was going to happen. I'm sure if you could have seen the future that you would have let Victor go a long time ago. Since you are not a clairvoyant, you just have to confront your demons and move on. You have to live with the decisions that you made. I think we both can agree that Victor is the one who is really having a hard time right now."

"But I still feel bad."

"Nique, you don't feel bad. True, you may wish that you were not going through all this with Kalil, but don't try that sob story crap with me. If you really felt bad, then you would have stopped screwing a married man long before it evolved into this." Alicia said point blank.

Monique was left thinking about the reality of Alicia's words. The truth of the matter was, she was only concerned about herself and her household. She was only sad because of the ill fate that her child had received. Her agony had nothing to do with Yvonne, or feeling bad for sharing her husband. She did feel that it was karma coming back to bite her.

For now, her energy had to be placed on the one who needed her the most. Dr. Anderson gave her a nutritious diet for Kalil and strict instructions to watch him for signs of worsening.

Yvonne awakened the next day with a screaming headache. She had cried herself to sleep. With the blinds pulled tightly, as not to awaken her, she was not sure what time it was. The sunlight was dancing around the blinds, peeking out of what little space there was. She vaguely even remembered coming back inside from the rain. She strained to focus her vision. Her clothes had dried by hanging over a chair during the course of her slumber.

Before she could find something to relieve her headache, she had to pull herself together. For a moment, she lay there hoping and praying that it would all go away, everything would be normal. She walked over to the sink and looked at her reflection. Her eyes were red and puffy. It had not gone away. She made herself look halfway presentable and thanked God above that Rosemary had convinced her to go to lunch. She put on her oversized Jackie O shades to hide her swollen eyes, which she left in her truck from the day before and drove to the nearest Wal-Mart.

Inside, she quickly picked up a few travel sized toiletries realizing that she had no intention on going home that day. She snatched two jogging suits and a casual capri and cotton T-shirt ensemble. Yvonne walked all the way to the check out line and had to back track to get something for her headache. Once she was finally settled, the young black Jackie O trudged the distance to her truck.

Normally, by this time, Yvonne would have gotten up, fixed Victor breakfast and or lunch, fed Kalia, gone for a walk with the New Mommies Club, showered and watched a talk show. This day was infinitely different.

Instead of having a nurturing breakfast of whole grains or fresh fruits, Yvonne stopped by Steak 'n' Shake for a brownie a la mode. She could not wait to get back into the hotel to tear into it.

She wanted a no stress day. Isolating herself to a hotel room where no one knew where she was and watching pay per view movies was as close as she would get. She tried to keep herself from thinking about the dismal truth that she was running away from.

Kalia's face was the only thing in that house Yvonne craved. She wanted to hold her and bathe her and watch her play around. She did not know whether Victor had gone to work and left Kalia with Rosemary or stayed at home with her. There was an easy way to find that out. She powered on her phone and called his office disguising her voice. Ms. Betsy was none the wiser when she told the caller that Victor was out of the office for the day.

Yvonne knew then that her husband had stayed home. She rolled her eyes knowing that if she wanted to check on her baby bundle, she would have to talk to him. Kalia was more important to than avoiding Victor. She knew what she had to do.

"Hello?" Victor jumped at the phone. He had been sitting on top of it since the moment Yvonne left.

"How is Kalia?" Yvonne said. Victor could hear her voice sounded weak.

"She's fine. She's taking a nap right now."

"Did she sleep okay?"

"Yes. Where are you?"

"What did you feed her for breakfast?" Her questions were rapid fire.

"Blueberry oatmeal, are you coming home?" He was obviously concerned but trying not to be too pushy. His manner with her was very easy.

"How long has she been asleep?" Yvonne was used to caring for her daughter and she had a schedule established.

"Oh, about 15 minutes. Baby..."

"Don't Baby me," she said curtly. The line went dead. Yvonne powered off her phone and continued her exile.

Victor was glad to hear from her. At least he knew that she was doing okay. He slipped into an old habit, calling her by a pet name. That was what ended the communication between them. He probably could have kept her on the phone for a little while longer. At this point, anything was better than nothing.

She turned on the T.V. in the hotel room and ordered a movie. She barely got through the credits before she started crying. Her life had suddenly become so overwhelming. The picture on the tube blurred through her mural of tears.

Yvonne wondered if Victor or Monique considered how this was going to affect her once she found out. She questioned how much longer would the affair have continued had Monique not become pregnant. It seemed to her that the guilty parties involved were only thinking about their lustful appetites and viewing the relationship through a kaleidoscope which allowed them to falsely believe that they were not really hurting anyone.

Since Yvonne was not talking to him, Victor opted to call the woman who would. Monique was going to be happy that he finally fessed up to his wife. He had not talked to her since they left Dr. Anderson's office. They both had a lot on their minds.

"How is Kalil doing?" He asked after Monique's salutation.

"He's doing alright. His urination is getting more frequent." They both knew what that meant.

"What about bleeding?"

"Every other diaper, which I guess is now more than before."

"Aww," she heard him whisper.

"How are things in your house?" He knew that Monique was prying.

"I told her about us...and Kalil..."

"And?"

"And my wife left." He said defeated. "She left the house and I have not seen her since."

"What do you mean you have not seen her since?" Monique felt her burden get lighter.

"Just what the hell I said. I told her all about us and she walked out of the front door. I don't know where she is or what she wants to do."

"Ouch."

"It's not like you care. You have made it no secret that you want her out of my life."

"Victor, I never said that."

"Not in so many words, but your actions always showed your true feelings. Let's not forget, neither of us is new to this."

"I'm sorry that things aren't on the up and up between you two." She sounded sincere, but Victor highly doubted that she was.

"Thanks." His acceptance was about as genuine as her apology.

"Why don't you come over?"

"I'm babysitting," he added quickly. Monique wasted no time slithering in to fill the void. He was not about to let that happen.

"Don't you think it's about time they met? They are brother and sister."

"No, I'll stay here and wait it out. The last thing I need is for Yvonne to come home and we aren't here." There was the sting. Monique's ego balloon began to deflate. The conversation ended quickly.

Yvonne felt like she had to talk to somebody. The only person she could think that would have the sense to offer any decent advice was Mary Louise. Mary Louise had proven herself to be worthy and Yvonne sought her counsel on every aspect of her life. Calling her was the natural thing to do.

"Mary Louise, I need to talk to you." The second Mrs. Parker heard Yvonne's voice, she knew that it was serious.

"Let me close my door." As she walked over to the door, she tried to imagine what was so pressing. Yvonne sounded nothing like herself. "Yvonne, I'm back."

Yvonne ensued in a soliloquy telling her everything about what happened between her and Victor and where she was. Mary Louise listened intently to the story as it unraveled itself. She closed her eyes not believing what was being said. Yvonne went into depth about how she had no family and had practically built her life around what she and Victor had.

Mary Louise's mind went to the day she found out that her husband had been cheating on her. The other woman came right out and told her that they were sharing Mr. Parker. The whole reason for the call was because the other woman was tired of sharing. She was doing the job that Mr. Parker did not want to. She knew that if she called his wife, that he would feel there was no need for him to hide around it anymore.

It took Mary Louise quite a long time to recover from the loss that she suffered. She worked for him and helped him build his business all for him to leave her and let some bimbo slide in right from under her nose. She knew firsthand the pain that Yvonne was feeling. What complicated Yvonne's situation was Kalia. Mary Louise did not have any children from Mr. Parker.

"It's okay to let it out," Mary Louise said hearing that Yvonne was trying to fight back her tears.

"I just don't know what to do. I am so confused. I did not deserve this."

"The good ones never do Honey," Mary Louise's tone was low and consoling.

"I just don't understand why he had to go do this to me. To us. Where did I go wrong?"

"You can't blame yourself, Yvonne. A person is going to do what a person is going to do. It's not your fault. If you live your life like there was something wrong with you, then you will in no ways recover."

"Mary Louise, I feel like my heart is going to fall out of my body."

"Understand one thing. I know firsthand what you feel, as far as him cheating on you for an extended period of time. If I could pull myself up and dust my knees off, so can you. You have more of a reason than I did. Yvonne, you have a precious baby who needs you." Mary Louise's words cut right through the quick.

"You're right," Yvonne sniffled, her face wet with tears.

"That girl does not have a weak mama. I raised you better than that." Yvonne smiled at the last remark. All of the real life skills that she used came directly from the school of Mary Louise Parker.

"How can I move forward? How can I look him in the eyes and know what he has done to me and it be alright?"

"Who said it had to be alright?"

"I don't want to get a divorce. I did not go into this marriage seeking a divorce."

"You don't have to get a divorce. What you do need to think about is whether or not you can look at him the same. I'm not telling you to go or to stay, I am saying that the decision is solely in your hands. Unless of course, he leaves you. After everything has died down, will you be able to trust Victor the same?"

"I don't know."

"One thing is for sure, you will not get any sort of resolution in that room."

"I had to get some time to myself."

"That's good, Baby. But if you don't know how to handle the situation, the only way to really be sure is to go back it. You have to look in his eyes when he talks to you."

"Thank you for talking to me," Yvonne's head was hurting even more. She lay on the bed looking at nothing in particular. The blinds were closed and the T.V. was off.

"Anytime, you call me if you need me. I mean that," Mary Louise added. Yvonne knew she meant it. If there was one word to describe Mary Louise and the relationship that the two ladies had developed over the years, it was true.

After another night in her secluded island of thought, Yvonne reconciled that Mary Louise was right, no progress was ever going to be made as long as she was away. She had to face the music. Her eyes had cried more tears in the last three days than the last three years combined. Her tear ducts were completely dry. She knew that if she needed to ever get away fast, that she had found a home in that hotel.
Yvonne gathered her things and prepared for the trip home. Every mile that the odometer counted was a change of heart. She was so undecided whether or not she really wanted to go home. Life was so peaceful in room 512. Every now and then a door would close loudly or there would be voices in the halls. For the most part, though, everything was great.
Her attention had to be on something else now, her marriage. If she was going to go back to her house, her mind had to be clear and focused. The instant she put her key in the lock, Victor knew it. Unbeknownst to each other, they both took deep breaths before the door opened. Yvonne did not know how she was going to act once she laid eyes on him. Victor had no idea of how to greet her. They were both going to play it by ear.
She walked in and was headed to the couch where Victor was holding Kalia. Kalia saw her mother and went crazy. She lunged for Yvonne and started telling her mother just how much she missed her, in baby talk of course. Yvonne spoke back letting her know that she was sorry for

leaving her and that she would not do it again. Victor did not know how to read that. It could have meant that she was not leaving. Contrary, it could have meant that if she did leave again, Kalia would be gone as well.

"I'm glad to know that you are okay," he started since the only real greeting they gave to one another was a head nod.

"I can take care of myself." Her words were dry. Victor knew he had some serious butt kissing to do if he were going to keep his home happy and together. He looked at his wife. She looked like she had a rough go of it lately. He did not want to dare ask.

"Are you hungry?"

"No," she smirked to herself thinking of her vacation diet of fast food and deserts. She sat on the floor and played with Kalia until they both fell asleep.

There was not much being said between the couple. Victor would ask the questions and Yvonne would give short and to the point responses. She took care of her daughter, feeding and changing her. Victor offered to put Kalia to bed and without saying a word, Yvonne handed the baby over and walked away. By the time he got Kalia bedded down for the night, he was ready for bed himself. He showered and did not see Yvonne. He hoped that she had not left again, going to check the living room. No Yvonne. He checked the office. No Yvonne. He checked the spare bedrooms. No Yvonne. He checked the loft with the daybed and there she lay.

"Yvonne, come to bed."

"I'm comfortable here," she insisted.

"Really, come on."

"Really, I'm comfortable."

"Please, Honey. I have not seen you for the past 3 days and you haven't said much of anything today. I cooked and you wouldn't eat my food. You won't even look at me. I know I messed up, but you can at least come to bed."

"You have no idea how bad you messed up. Why would I want to share a bed with you? You have totally defiled our bed." She sat up and looked at him. The streetlight was enlightening one side of his face as he stood in the doorway.

"I never did anything in that bed," he said pointing towards their room downstairs. "I would never do that."

"But you would still have sex with someone else. So... why don't you invite her to the bed with you since whatever I was doing wasn't good enough."

"Yvonne, you are so wrong."

"So tell me. Tell me why you had an affair Victor." She crossed her arms and waited to hear what excuse he was going to come up with. Regardless of what it was, it still would not be sufficient.

"I don't know." He hung his head maintaining his composure.

"Victor," Yvonne began to raise her voice, "you come to me and tell me that you have been having an affair that resulted in an illegitimate child and all you have to say is you don't know? You better come up with something better than that! Tell me why you did it?"

"Yvonne, she threw herself at me." He responded like a kid who was being scolded.

"You weren't man enough to stand up for your family? Just like that, a woman threw herself at you and you fell for it? How many times did it take 1, 2, 10? Did she really even throw herself at you or was it the other way around?" She stood up.

"She threw herself at me and I don't know why I didn't stop her." He had to take whatever Yvonne was about to give him. He had to let her get her frustration out or they could never move forward.

"Why didn't you stop her? Why did you keep having sex with her? You couldn't get her out of your system? You Jonesin' for her, huh? Is that it?!" Yvonne was slowly making her way over to him.

"No Yvonne. I never intended for it to get to this point."

"But it did and what have you done about it? Nothing! You stood there and did nothing! You are out there risking my life having sex with some nasty skank and not even thinking about me! Did you ever think about me, Victor?" It pained him the way she kept making the argument personal. She was right in his face now. If Monique was pulling this stunt, he would have pushed her out of his face long before she got this close. He had never seen Yvonne like this before.

"Yes."

"Oh," she said mock laughing, "so you thought about me. Was that before or after you were between her legs?"

"Yvonne," he started, but he had nothing to say.

"Yvonne what? Are you going to tell me you love me? I hope not because that is not what I want to hear right now."

"What do you want to hear, Yvonne?" He personalized it for her.

"I want to hear the truth!" The ducts that she thought were dry, somehow began to squeeze out tears. "I want you to tell me that I am not enough for you! I want you to tell me that you want to go have another family with another woman! I want you to tell me that you are going to be able to look at Kalia in her eyes when she gets older and tell her not to marry a man like you who can't keep his penis in his pants! I want you to tell me the real reason why you stepped out on me because, I don't know, isn't cutting it!"

By the time she finished, she was almost doubled over, holding herself. Victor caught himself with tears streaming down his own face. He tried to hold her, she screamed at him. He put his back to the wall and slid down until he was sitting on the floor. She sat back on the bed. They just sat there looking at each other through teary walls.

"I do love you," she saw the silhouette of his mouth moving. "I am so sorry about all of it. There is no excuse for it. Leaving you," she could hear the emotion building back up, "was never part of the plan. Keeping you and Kalia happy was always my number one priority."

Yvonne sniffled. Victor sniffled. She massaged her temples with her hands. She looked at the man she loved so much. She knew that their home would not be happy for a long time to come. They were probably going to have several more blow outs before it was all over with.

"Why did you buy me a new truck."

"To be honest..."

"I don't think that's a good way to begin a sentence," she interrupted.

"I decided to buy you that truck the day you suggested it. I wanted to make it more special than you just asking and receiving. That's why I came up with the elaborate early anniversary celebration."

"Okay." Yvonne laid her head down on the day bed and stuffed a pillow underneath her. Realizing that her first night home would not be a night that she spent with him, Victor found a pillow and laid down on the floor next to the bed. He did not want to sleep in their bed alone.

The next day, by the time he woke up, she was gone. He looked at the bed, there was nobody there. He went downstairs and found her feeding Kalia while watching the news. He told her that he had to go into the office, even if just for half a day since he had been home for the last 3 days. In a barely responsive voice, she told him to stay there all day and that there was no need for him to come home.

As soon as he got to the office, from being out sick with a stomach flu, his co-workers stopped by the office to check on him. He managed to call a local florist and have an order of flowers sent to Yvonne at the house. He had to show some type of apologetic venture. He had to do more than just say he was sorry, he had to show her felt that way too.

When Rosemary and Susan stopped by at the appointed time, Yvonne told them that she would not be walking. They wanted to probe and find out where she had been for the last couple days. They wanted her to volunteer some information. They did not get either resolution that they hoped for.

"Did you see her?" Susan asked Rosemary as they began their walk.

"Yeah," Rosemary said shaking her head.

"She looks really bad. I wonder what is going on in there."

"Whatever it is, she doesn't want us to know."

"How do you know Rosemary? She could be hoping that we reach out to her. She's probably hoping that we would ask her."

"If Yvonne wants to talk, she'll let you know."

"I think maybe we should try to help her."

"Oh Susan, you aren't trying to help. You are poking your nose where it doesn't belong. Now pick up your pace, you're slowing me down." That was Rosemary's way of telling Susan to hush. When Rosemary did find out what was going on in the house next door, she made it a point not to tell Susan. The only way that Susan would find out was if Yvonne herself told her.

Yvonne got the flowers Victor sent to her and left them right by the door. She did not bother to take them inside or give them a nice home. The little table in the hall held the vase and the mail stock piled for the last 3 days, since Victor never went through it.

Her day flew by, being home at peace with her princess. The minute that Victor came home, the tension started. It was a big pink elephant in the room. For some reason, Victor had his fingers crossed that he would walk in the house and smell dinner cooking. To him it would symbolize that everything was somewhat back to normal or on its way there. The only thing he smelled when he walked in the house was Tropical Breeze air freshener.

Their talking was very minimal, only the necessary conversation. This was going to be a long weekend. Yvonne did not say anything about the flowers. Normally, she would have called to thank him. He thought that maybe he could get Yvonne out of the house and somewhat lighten the mood between them. All that would probably do was make the distance between them more apparent. He did not want to do anything that would widen the gap.

Yvonne took care of that for him. Saturday morning, she made breakfast for herself and her child. She got them both ready and told Victor they were headed to the mall. When he relayed that he wanted to go, Yvonne told him she and Kalia were already set to go and left. She drove nearly an hour to the Lenox Mall and strolled Kalia around. They perused ever so casually around the bottom floor, then the top. Yvonne bought a few things for them both, forgetting all about Daddy.

She left that mall and went to the Cheesecake Factory. Since, by that time it was the middle of a Saturday, there was a waiting line. By the time they got home it was well into the afternoon. They were both tired. Yvonne took a nap and so did Kalia.

Victor felt so lonesome. He hoped that they could hurry and get past this stage because he did not want to have too many more weeks like this one. He spent half of the week without even laying eyes on his wife, let alone talk to her. The talking they did was all argumentative. Things were not the same. She had not been there to make his breakfast, meet him at the door when he got home or cook him dinner.

The life that Victor had been half-heartedly trying to protect was collapsing before his eyes. His marriage, their friendship, his relationship with Kalia. It killed him to think that he might not be able to wake up in the same house as Kalia. A strained relationship with Yvonne ultimately meant a strained relationship with their daughter.

It would take him a whole lifetime to find another wife like Yvonne. Further more, what woman in her right mind would want to be with him after hearing the entire truth? Trust is something that he would lack from all angles of his life. Sitting at the house without Yvonne and Kalia, he thought about the future of his family. He had no say in what happened, it was up to his wife to forgive him.

Yvonne was the best wife that he could have asked for and he had taken all of the things she did for him for granted. He thought that, well, he really was not thinking, if he knew then, he would have never touched Monique. That night, the routine was the same. When it came time to go to bed, Yvonne found herself in the loft. Victor knew the reason that she chose the loft instead of the guest bed room was because that bed was not big enough for them both.

"Baby come to bed," he tried again.

"I'm in bed."

"This is not our bed."

"You did not honor our bed and I don't want to sleep there."

"I did not sleep with anybody but you in our bed." Yvonne looked up at him. He knew she was speaking figuratively and he was speaking literally.

"But you have been with somebody else."

"Please don't start this again, tonight. Let's go to sleep."

"I'm not starting anything. You came in here messing with me."

"Yvonne, come on. We need to stay a family for Kalia."

"Family? Oh, now you want to think about family. What about being a family for Kalil?" He opened the door and she walked in. The tears began to roll.

"Me, you and Kalia are a family."

"Are you saying that Kalil is not your family? He's your flesh and blood, isn't he?" Looking him straight in his eye, she started to shake. The moon was high and she could see his face fully. Victor looked out of the window. He had no rebuttal. Kalil was indeed part of his family. He had two children now.

"Yvonne, I want us to rebuild."

"Rebuild what, the lie that we were living before?" Her words were sharp, but they had all the truth in the world.

"Rebuild us, what we had."

"I don't know if I can look at you and trust anything that you say to me. How can I believe what comes out of your mouth? What makes me think that after 3 or 4 years of keeping secrets, you can go back to being truthful?"

"The reason that I came out and told you is because I knew I had to for us to make forward progress."

"See, you're lying already. The reason that you told me is because that boy is sick and you had no other choice!" She rolled over, with her back facing him standing there and wiped her eyes. She felt like getting up and running out of the house. She wanted to run back to her serene hotel room. Part of being an adult, a real woman, was facing problems head on.

Victor had to let it go. He had lost the fight a second night. He exhaled, grabbed his pillow and blanket, lying down beside her on the floor.

Chapter 12

"I think that we should have Kalia tested to be a donor for Kalil." Monique blasted into the phone. "His bleeding is getting heavier. If we wait for a donor to die, then Kalil could die in the process, or his quality of living will be so poor that he can't have the surgery."

"I'll have to talk to Yvonne about that." Victor was living and breathing the repercussions of his transgression everyday.

"Do what you need to do, your son is sick."

"I'll talk to her about it. I'll warn you though, its not very likely that she'll want to do it."

"You need to make her do it."

"Its not that simple. I am not going to do anything that Kalia's mother isn't going for. I'll talk to her about it."

"If you don't, I will."

"I've already told you about threatening me. Calm your ass down. I will ask my wife."

How did Monique expect him to go to his wife asking her to save his illegitimate child? All hell was really about to break loose. He put his hands over his face. He spun his chair around to look out of the window.

Jumping seemed like the only viable option. The only problem was his office was on the third floor. If he jumped, he probably would not do enough damage to put him completely out of the game. He had to draw some strength from somewhere. Any other time, Yvonne would have been that for him, now he needed strength to face her.

He had been running from all this for a while. Regardless of how he did not feel like approaching Yvonne with the question of using their child as a donor, it was possibly the quickest way for Kalil to heal. If the little rascal still did not make it after that, at least Victor could say that he tried.

The rest of the day inched by. It seemed that he was hitting Yvonne with one blow after another. He knew that this was going to be pushing it over the top. How could he ask her to risk her child's life to save one who should not even exist? He found himself asking lots of questions lately. There were no answers that made any sense. Yvonne was asking him all the questions that he had been asking himself. The only difference was when he asked himself, he did not have to have an answer. He would just shrug his shoulders and figure that he would worry about it later.

"Yvonne!" He called out into the house.

"Yes," he found her in the rocking chair.

"There has been a new development."

"Can my life take any more turns?" Her face looked like she was overwhelmed. As she was.

"Monique wants to know if you will allow Kalia to be tested as a donor."

"A donor for what?" Yvonne snapped.

"A donor for Kalil."

"What? Is she for real? Are you for real coming to me with this crap? Why would I want to let my child save that boy's life? He can wait for all I care."

"He's innocent in all this, Yvonne." Victor was giving her the most pathetic look possible.

"So is Kalia. What if she's allergic to the anesthesia and her whole system shuts down? What if she never comes out of recovery? Are me and Monique supposed to share her son who took my daughter's life."

"You're being irrational."

"Irrational my ass! Did you even think about what you were saying before you said it? I don't think so!" Yvonne's raised voice awakened Kalia. She started screaming. Yvonne rushed passed him to go comfort the baby. He casually followed her into the next room.

"Why should Kalil have to suffer?"

"He won't suffer for long if they hurry and put his name on the list." She was talking over the cries. Yvonne began pacing, bouncing their daughter up and down to calm her.

Victor knew that was the reaction that he was going to get. He was determined to try again. He knew sooner or later, she was bound to give in and do the right thing. Hopefully that time would not be too far away.

"Yvonne, I miss you. I miss us. When are we going to go back to the way we used to be?"

"Now you miss me. You didn't appreciate me when you had me." She did not even bother to look at him. Her attention was instead on Kalia who was slowly winding down. Victor headed to the kitchen, which had almost become unfamiliar territory to him. He cooked fried fish and grits. It was a quick and easy meal. Once he was done, he set the table for two like Yvonne always did. She by passed the table and got a banana out of the refrigerator.

"Yvonne what's with you?" He slammed down a cup on the counter. "I'm tired of this. You aren't talking to me, when you do, you are short with me. You sleep in the loft so you can sleep by yourself. You are acting like I'm a pariah!"

"One week ago, my husband told me that he cheated on me and had a baby by one of his office staff. If that wasn't enough, he asked me to let my child be the donor to save the other child's life. Victor, if you can't see the magnitude of that would tear a person apart, then you aren't the man I married."

"I understand you're hurt, but..."

"But what? You are all that I have. I loved you, I honored you, I was a good wife."

"Was?" It caught him by surprise.

"I thought I knew how to treat my man. I thought that cooking him dinner, even after I had worked all day, was my job. I thought breaking him off with sex when he wanted, was my job. I thought buying him gifts for no reason other than I wanted to, was my job. Apparently, loving him as long and hard as I did was not enough. No, you don't understand my hurt. Your wife never tipped out on you or gave you a reason to suspect anything."

He was left speechless. Yvonne was right. This time, she was not crying. She was finding her inner strength from somewhere. Kalia had straightened up though it was clear that she was still irritated.

"Let me rephrase. I know that I hurt you and I do apologize. I don't know what I can do to make you see that the real reason why I ended the affair last year was because I was tired of fooling around."

"Or you were mad because she wouldn't have the abortion that you wanted her to have. You should not have married me if you weren't done fooling around. I did not put any pressure on you." They stood looking into each other's eyes.

Victor searched Yvonne's eyes for a hint of forgiveness which she had yet to verbally assign. He looked for the pieces of their future that he used to see. He wanted to catch a glimpse of happiness. Her eyes had not danced in a long time. In calendar days, it was more like 7, but in emotional sunrises and sunsets, it seemed like the time was endless.

Yvonne almost could not reach back to the time when they were a normal family, a happy couple. In Victor's eyes, she hunted for truth, some sort of resolution. All that both of them saw were blank, open stares. Life was not fair.

"Not today girls," Yvonne turned Susan and Rosemary down for her morning walk again.

"Surely you can come out for a walk," Susan said.

"I'm just not up to it," Yvonne forced.

"Yvonne, I'm putting my foot down," Rosemary said. "You need to come out with us. We miss you and you must get out of this house." Yvonne knew they just wanted her to feel better. She appreciated them not digging too deep to find out the real cause. She certainly did not want to burden them with the realities of her miserable life.

"I can't."

"I think you should. Look at you," Susan motioned. "Your hair has been in a messy ponytail for days. You look like you haven't gotten any sleep in a month and nothing to eat all week!" Yvonne had not noticed how disheveled her appearance looked.

"The last two days we came to check on you, you had on the same outfit," Rosemary added.

"I'm just lounging around the house," Yvonne said in her defense.

"In the same outfit? We know something's up. Sometimes it just helps to get out and get some fresh air." Susan was coaxing her out of the house.

"Thanks, but no thanks. Not today."

"Well then, we'll just come in your dungeon with you." Rosemary pushed past Yvonne and drove her stroller with Jackson in tow into the foyer of the house. Susan followed. Before Yvonne could oppose, both of her neighbors were inside her house.

Rosemary found her way around the kitchen and fixed the ladies a light lunch. The kids enjoyed playing with each other, as usual. During the course of their visit the phone rang several times. Yvonne did not bother to answer it, instead letting the answering machine talk to her callers.

Rosemary made some sandwiches and mimosas. They watched T.V. all afternoon long. By the time they looked up, school buses were rolling through their neighborhood. Susan and Rosemary excused themselves so they could get dinner on the stove for their husbands.

Yvonne was thankful that they came, but at the same time, they took up all of her peace time. The only time when she felt at ease to be in a relaxed state of mind was when Victor was at work. He would be home much sooner than later now. At least Kalia had a good time playing with Jackson and Little Charles.

The phone rang again and she figured that she might as well answer it. She knew that it was probably her husband on the other end. What he wanted she was not sure. Whatever it was, it could have waited until he got home.

"Hello."

"May I speak to Yvonne." Yvonne did not recognize the voice.

"Speaking."

"Hi, this is Monique." The phone went dead. No sooner than Yvonne heard the name, she ended the call. Her heart started beating fast and she felt flushed. She could not believe that Monique had the nerve to call her house. What in the world did they have to talk about? The phone rang again.

"Don't you ever call my house again!" Yvonne yelled into the receiver and disconnected the line again. She was flustered. She could not believe that Monique had the nerve to call her. Anything Monique needed to say, she could say it through Victor. As far as her having the audacity to call his wife, she was over stepping her bounds.

Monique knew she was treading on shaky ground. She hoped that by talking to Yvonne woman to woman, she could convince the other young lady to have her daughter tested. Monique wanted Yvonne to hear it from her. She wanted it done right and knew she had to do it herself. She called again.

"Don't hang up the phone!" Monique said quickly. "I just want to talk to you."

"What do we have to talk about?"

"I know that I am probably the last person you want to talk to."

"You have a lot of nerve calling me."

"I want to talk to you face to face."

"Oh hell no! That is not going to happen sweetie. It's not enough that you've already been sexing Victor, now you wanna harass me about it?" Monique had to let the talk go over her head. She knew what she was doing when she called Yvonne.

"I would like to talk to you about our children."

"That's fine. I don't need any help with mine. You can get all the help you need from Victor. We are not about to start some happy family threesome," Yvonne snapped.

"Please, Yvonne, I think we have a lot to learn from one another." Yvonne hung up the phone. Not only did Victor's girlfriend call her at home and suggest that they meet, she also insulted her by saying they had lots to learn from each other.

Yvonne got on the phone and called Victor right away. He knew something drastic must have happened for his wife who was barely speaking to him to be calling him. Drastic was right.

"Your damn girlfriend just called me, Victor! Its bad enough I have to deal with the infidelity, but I don't need it in my face! You need to get a handle on that girl!" Yvonne screamed into the receiver. Victor was heated. *I told her that I was going to talk to Yvonne myself,* he thought. He called Monique as soon as he got off the phone with Yvonne. Monique was trying to play the innocent role. He knew much better than that.

She said that she would not have had to call Yvonne if Victor had done what he was supposed to do. Victor went off on her. Monique was just burning her bridges with them both. Victor was the main person that she need not mess up with. He was trying to hang in there and be supportive of her through it all. He would not stand by and allow her to pester his wife.

Monique was barred from calling Yvonne. Still, she had to get to her any way she could. She sat in her living room watching her child play. The thought that he could be taken away from her was devastating. The more and more she thought about it, she felt that she had to try again.

Monique was desperate for some help to save the life of her infant son. Monique thought that she could summon the maternal instinct of Yvonne better than her husband could. Monique opted to give the connection one more try.

"My son is dying and your daughter could possibly save his life," Monique began as soon as Yvonne answered the phone. "I would really like the opportunity to talk to you face to face so you can hear my plea. We can meet anywhere. You name the time and place, we'll be there."

Yvonne thought about it for a second. If she agreed to meet Monique, then maybe she would quit calling Yvonne. In the same token, meeting her would put a face with a name. Yvonne preferred not to know what her husband's lover looked like. At least this would shut her up. It was either meet the crazy wench or have her start stalking the house.

"Piedmont Park, tomorrow, at umm, 11."

"Thank you so much," Monique sounded eternally grateful.

"I'll be wearing…"

"I know what you look like. See you then." Monique was finally satisfied. She managed, through several attempts, to reach Yvonne. At last, she was heard without Yvonne yelling or hanging up. Now, she had less than 24 hours to plan her position. She had to make sure not to say anything that would offend Yvonne. This was a very sensitive time for her.

Monique really could not even imagine what Yvonne must be feeling, agreeing to see the woman who slept with her husband. She had to give Yvonne credit where it was due. It took a real woman to do what she was about to do.

Yvonne, on the other hand, was trying to figure out what was going through her mind when she was on the phone. The last thing she needed was to put a face with a name. She could have cared less what Monique looked like. Seeing her would do nothing less than put an image in her head of Monique and Victor having sex. She was going to be sick to her stomach.

Yvonne, still sleeping in the loft with Victor on the floor, did not get a good nights sleep that night. She tossed and turned all night. She spent a good part of the night looking just above the blinds at the moonlight peering through. Her mind was going a million miles a minute. The next day, she mentally prepared herself for the task of talking to this woman.

Neither of them had breathed a word to Victor. Monique did not tell him because she presumed that Yvonne would. Yvonne did not because she had already sent Victor to talk to Monique and it did no good since Monique called her again anyway. If Yvonne wanted to get rid of Monique, she had to do it herself.

Yvonne arrived at the park early. She made sure that she and her daughter were tightly wrapped up before stepping into the early winter weather. She walked with 7 month old Kalia in her arms and found a seat on a bench. She was so nervous. She really had no reason to be. Facing the woman who had tried to break up her marriage was enough in itself.

Monique was the one who should have been nervous. She was approaching the woman whose life was falling apart, to a degree because of her. On top of that, she was asking for an act of kindness that would hold two precious lives in her hands. Seeing a young, black lady walking towards her, Yvonne knew it was Monique. Her heart was in her throat.

"Thank you for meeting with me," Monique said. She held out her hand to shake it and Yvonne just looked at the hand then back at her face.

"Ok."

"This is Kalil," Monique began proudly. She offered him to Yvonne so that she could get a better look. Yvonne held Kalia tighter. She was holding her baby over her shoulder away from Monique.

"I did not agree to meet with you to become bosom buddies." Yvonne said dryly.

"You're right. Victor said that he was going to talk to you about Kalia being a donor for Kalil."

"He did."

"He never said anything else to me about it other than he felt like he had no right to ask you to have her tested since he was in the wrong."

"As far as I'm concerned, you're both wrong. He talked to me about getting her tested. I'm just not so sure that's a good idea."

"Why not?" Monique was being very direct.

"My daughter had nothing to do with your son."

"They are brother and sister."

"That has nothing to do with me," Yvonne said feeling nothing for Kalil.

"But you can do something about it. I know you are aware of the kind of illness that my son has. You also know that both parents have to have the trait in order for the child to have the disease. If your background is clean, then Kalia could very well be able to donate one of her kidneys to Kalil."

"Please forgive me if saving your son's life is not on my list of things to do. You slept with my husband and you knew that he was married. That did not stop you from flaunting your ass all around him."

"With all due respect, he could have turned me down Yvonne."

"Do you not have any respect for yourself? How does it make you feel to know that you can't get men on your own so you have to try to take other women's men? Then you have the nerve to ask me to risk my child's life to save yours."

"Yvonne, we can go back and forth about mine and Victor's relationship, but that would not do very much good. We are here to talk about the children."

"Your child...who was conceived out of adultery." Yvonne's words cut Monique deep. She could not deny what they both knew to be true.

"Think back to the day you found out you were pregnant. You were excited and started planning the child's future long before you knew the sex. You imagined what she would look like, what type of personality she would have. I'm sure once you found out it was a girl, you could not wait until she got old enough for you to hang out together, go shopping together."

"Imagine all of that," Monique continued, "was taken away from you at the blink of an eye. Imagine that your hopes of your little girl growing up and going through school are all erased because she's sick. Now imagine that you know a way to save her life while preserving her quality of life. Yvonne that's where I am. If I can find a donor, Kalil won't have to wait on the list for a kidney and his illness won't get significantly worse."

"Kalia might not even be a match and you are going through all of this for nothing."

"But at least we can say we tried. I'm a mother talking to you as a mother. You would do anything you could to save her."

"You keep forgetting that I'm still digesting the whole betrayal that took place."

"I'm not forgetting that. I'm not asking you to do this for me or for Victor. I'm asking you to do this for an innocent child whose life you can save."

"I'm just not so sure that..."

"We can set up an appointment with the doctor to assess the risk to your daughter, which I'm sure is minimal. I don't think he would have suggested it if the procedure was risky." Yvonne was shaking her head at Monique. She did have a point, the baby was totally innocent. It was not Kalil's fault that he was birthed into this crazy mess.

"You are very persistent."

"Do you know how I found out that my baby was sick?" Monique looked Yvonne in the eyes, "there was blood in his urine. Please get Kalia tested."

"Okay, okay." Yvonne finally gave up the ghost. Monique was excited but very humbled thinking how painful all this must be for Yvonne.

"Thank you so much." Monique said and the ladies went on their way. For the first time ever, Monique felt sorry for what she had done to Yvonne. Yvonne was just a normal young female trying to make her marriage work. She had not bargained for all that she got in addition.

The drive back to Fayetteville was a long one. Yvonne needed to get it all out, she needed to talk to someone who was not involved in the triangle. She needed an outside opinion. The entire ride home, she kept looking at the little one, in the back seat who had not a single clue of all the confusion that was going on around her. Once she got home, Yvonne went over to see Rosemary.

She opened up her heart and told her about the whole episode from beginning to end. Gratefully, she had Rosemary's undivided attention. Rosemary was beside herself. She could not believe that Victor had let it go on as far as he had. She wondered if there could ever be anything such as a devoted husband. Yvonne talked and talked, she cried and cried. Rosemary listened to the whole story and comforted her neighbor and friend. Then she decided to open up and tell a little story of her own.

Rosemary and Tom had been married for about ten years. Rosemary told Yvonne the tale of how her husband, Tom, had cheated on her. The pattern started slowly. The common signs of staying late at work, not being there when he was supposed to be and hanging out after work were all there. She ignored them. Their sex life was still the same as it had always been, so Rosemary admitted that she did not consider anything phony about his work schedule.

Then she became pregnant with their first child after two years. Yvonne looked puzzled. She knew about Jackson, but she had never heard anything about another child. As the story continued, the pregnancy went on without a hitch and their daughter, Amber, was born. Life was great in the Blevins household. The family was a happy, new family.

Tom started rushing home after work instead of picking up extra shifts at the pharmacy. Rosemary cooked dinner almost every night and they spent all Tom's free time together. Being a stay-at-home-mom was right up her alley. Then one day, she went to check Amber during her nap. She was not breathing.

"I walked in her room to check on her. I put my hand on her back," Rosemary's face got flushed describing how her daughter died. "She did not move. I turned her over and her little body just flopped in my hands." The tears in Rosemary's eyes let her neighbor know that she was not making this story up. Almost the entire time that she was talking, she was looking down at the floor. Having eye contact would only make the narrative harder.

"I picked her up and tried to shake her a little. There was absolutely no response. I ran into the next room and called 911. They pronounced her in my living room."

"Rosemary," Yvonne tried to console her, "I had no idea."

"It's not something that you will ever hear me talk about. She was my first child and that was an extremely tough time for us. The hardest part was calling Tom. He was beside himself."

"What took her?"

"SIDS...It was SIDS..." Rosemary's eyes stared blankly into the floorboard. She went on to declare that day to be the worst day of her life. Yvonne had no clue, Rosemary never talked about Amber. She then told Yvonne that the reason why she did not discuss Amber is because it was too painful.

Tom did not blame his wife, but she always felt that he did. She could not forgive herself, Amber died on her watch. Due to Rosemary's worsening depression, her husband stayed to himself a lot. The gap between them eventually turned into an ocean. He would work double shifts, she would sleep all day long and not get out of bed. They went through a very tough few months.

As Rosemary begin to come back around, she found out that Tom was having an affair with one of his customers. The pain was unbearable. Instead of her coming out of her depression, she sank further down. For about the next year, she and her husband lived practically as roommates. He was still supporting them and she was acting as a chef and maid. Having sex became almost repulsive. They did not touch each other.

Yvonne listened intently. Rosemary told her that one day, she realized that she absolutely, positively had to get some help. She suggested to Tom that she see counseling and told him to either help her get better or divorce her. When it was all said and done, they worked things out and now, they are a brand new couple.

"So you see Yvonne, no marriage is a crystal stair. Things happen. You have to decide if you want to stay with Victor. If you do stay, can you look at him everyday and know that he did not honor your vows? If you don't stay, can you see him with another woman and their children? It's no easy decision, but its one that you have to make."

Yvonne sat there for a moment and listened to her friend. Everything that Rosemary said to her made sense. The choice was going to be up to her. If Victor wanted out, he would have left when everything surfaced. It was apparent that he did not have a desire to leave just in the manner in which he slept. His palate was on the floor next to Yvonne every night.

Marriage was something very sacred and hers had been violated. What was worse was the fact that her husband's indiscretion was not just going to skimp away. Every time she thought about Kalil, she was reminded that it would not easily go away. The decision was not going to be easy.

Yvonne told Victor about her meeting with Monique and that she was going to let Kalia be tested. Victor was thankful and tried to hug Yvonne. She stepped away. She let it be known that she was not doing it for him or Monique. What was eating her up was knowing that she could very well be able to save that baby's life and she was holding out.

As promised, Yvonne went to see Dr. Anderson to have Kalia tested. She also asked the good doctor a host of questions to ensure that her child would be safe. After all of her anxieties were calmed, the doctor performed the sample collection that he needed. He told her that he would get the results as soon as possible.

When the results came back, they were delivered to Yvonne by Dr. Anderson. His heart went out to Yvonne. He could see during their consultations how burned she was by the whole scenario. Nobody deserved to go through what she had gone through. He let her know that Kalia was a positive match for her sibling, Kalil.

The reason that he decided to disclose the news to her and her alone, is because he wanted her to have time to process the information herself, alone. He wanted her to have time to think about exactly what she was going to do without Monique pleading and Victor insisting that the kidney donation take place.

After he gave her the test results, he got the response that he anticipated. Silence. Now, Yvonne was stuck between a rock and a hard place. She knew that she could possibly save this innocent boy's life. The catch was, she did not feel that it was her duty to do. His whole existence should never have come to being. The last thing in the world she wanted to do was be obligated to help her husband's lover with her problems.

Chapter 13

Yvonne told her husband that Kalia was a donor match. He was excited, but tried to hide it. They had only won a portion of the battle. Now, Yvonne had to be convinced that sharing Kalia was the right thing to do. There was also the realization that Kalil still might reject his sister's kidney.

Of course, Victor was quick to call Monique and tell her the news. She yelled loud through the house. Her prayers were being answered. She picked up her son and told him that his sister was a match and she was going to save his life. Kalil giggled. He was happy because his mother was happy.

Dr. Anderson made an appointment with the three of them. The Russell family arrived first. They were escorted to the doctor's office to wait on the extended family. When Monique arrived, Kalil saw his father and held out his arms for Victor to take him.

"Da Da," he spoke. Yvonne closed her eyes tightly. Dr. Anderson watched Yvonne, he was very sensitive to her. She felt like crying and running out, but Yvonne knew she had to keep her act together. They were here for a reason.

There they sat. Victor was in the middle. On his left was Monique with her son sitting on her lap. On his right was his wife who was keeping an eye on their daughter in a stroller. Kalia was fast asleep.

"As we all know, Kalia is a very good donor match for Kalil," Dr. Anderson's head was tilted toward his desk, but his eyes were glancing over the top of his glasses.

"How many other donors do we need to have tested?" Monique asked.

"That depends on what Mrs. Russell decides to do." Monique shot the doctor a nasty look.

"Mrs. Russell," Monique said with a twinge to her tone, "what are you going to do?"

"Now is not the time to get salty with me." Yvonne spoke up.

"Dr. Anderson, how soon would you recommend performing the surgery?" Victor wanted to break up the scene.

"In his last check-up, Kalil had developed hemorrhoids and an elevated blood pressure. He is also noticeably smaller than his sister who is the exact same age."

"Can't that be attributed to genetics?" Yvonne asked. Dr. Anderson knew that before it was over, there would surely be a cat fight in his office. He hated to do this consultation, but he wanted to see Kalil through to the end.

"Yes and no. Yes, some children are bigger than others, no in that at this early stage in the game, growth is pretty much even across the board. He is growing, but not at the pace I would expect him to. That's because his kidneys are not functioning properly."

"Do you think that it's really necessary to have the surgery with them being this young, Dr. Anderson?"

"Any surgery has its risks, but I wholly think that they will recover quite nicely. Kalia will obviously have the least amount of risk. Kalil is the one who will have more complications. His body may reject the kidney which can happen instantaneously or over time. The final option is that he can accept the kidney and go on to live a perfectly normal, healthy life." He added the last bit with such opulence that they were all hopeful.

"How long will the surgery take?" Monique continued.

"I'd say a good couple of hours. We have to remove his kidneys, then harvest a fresh kidney from Kalia and give it to Kalil."

"Harvest?" Yvonne did not like the way that sounded.

"It sounds a lot worse than it really is." Dr Anderson tried to convince her.

"How long will it take Kalil to recover?" Victor was concerned.

"That depends on him and how well his body accepts the kidney."

"And you suspect that he will be fine with the donor kidney?" It was becoming a two person conversation between the two men in the room.

"I do. I have no reason to think otherwise. His condition is not so far gone that his health will be in very imminent danger."

"In the event that he does reject it, what is the process then?"

"His name will go on a waiting list."

"How long is that list?"

"Surprisingly not very long. There are not many babies of 7 months who need kidneys. The down side to that is there are not many healthy babies of 7 months who can yield their kidneys upon death." The tone of the room turned somber. Hearing the words babies and death in the same sentence did nothing for the vibes in the room.

"I understand that the sooner the better for him to have the surgery. I'm just not so sure that I am ready to commit my little girl to something like this."

"Please Yvonne, for the sake of my only son," Victor echoed from the depths of his heart. Yvonne looked at her husband with a look of confusion. Dr. Anderson and Monique were quiet, the moment was clearly between The Russells. Yvonne could not believe what had just come out of Victor's mouth.

"For the sake of your only son?" She whispered with tears brimming in her eyes. "You bastard," she slapped him and stood up. She wiped the tears from her cheeks and pushed the stroller out of the office.

Victor hung his head. He was speaking emotionally, making the comment before even realizing it. He should have been able to see her concern, but his mind was on saving the life of his child. What little progress he had made with his wife had quickly turned into regression.

He put his hand on the back of his own neck and thanked Dr. Anderson for his time. He told the doctor that they would be in touch. Victor realized, after his wife left, that it was going to be virtually impossible for him to take care of Kalil and keep his marriage afloat. Yvonne was too wounded. One of the relationships was going to be lacking, he wanted that for neither.

Victor would have to put forth a concerted effort on his part to make things work between him and both women. Although his wife was more important, Monique was still the mother of his child. Regardless of whether or not Yvonne was happy with the situation, Kalil was going to be a part of Victor's life. He wanted the best for his child and right now that consisted of getting him to live.

When Victor arrived at his house, Yvonne was balled up on a beanbag on the floor. He sat down next to her and stroked her head working his hand from her scalp to the curled ends. She wanted to buck and not let him touch her, but it had been so long. She was still very much in love with her husband and missed the times when they would simply spend time together.

It seemed that they could not even talk about current events going on in the world without it leading to Monique and Kalil. One way or another, everything lead back to that. His hands ran smoothly through the big curls that were roller set into her hair. He loved her hair that way. It looked so classic.

Just being that close to him bought out emotion. She was so torn, love…hate…betrayal…forgiveness… justified. Victor had turned her into a person that she did not even recognize. She did not know where the sweet, gentile Yvonne had gone. Her life had not been this complicated in a very, very, long time. He sensed everything that she was feeling. He bent down and kissed her on the forehead. She wanted to buck again, but she was frozen. She had forgotten what it felt like to be touched, caressed.

Victor was her husband. With his hand, he sweetly brushed the tear from her face. Then there was another. He brushed it away. He took the tips of his fingers and gently massaged her scalp. She unwound some of the tension by letting him take her away. Apologizing was not going to make it go away. Denying it was not going to make it disappear. He had to hit it head on, which he was finally doing.

Speaking would ruin the moment, the intimacy. He had worked too hard over the last couple of weeks with no positive return. Yvonne got flowers every other day, hot meals prepared that she would not eat. He slept on the floor and spent more time with Kalia to give Yvonne the space he knew she needed.

The shadow of the bookcase from the sun was sliding down the wall. It was evident that time was passing them by. Neither one of them wanted to move or say anything. Yvonne still had unanswered questions and curiosities. But his touch. Somehow with his touch, he was trying to make it right.

"I almost don't believe Dr. Anderson when he says that everything is going to be okay." Monique told Alicia.

"Why not?"

"I don't know. They are just so young. How can this surgery go off without a hitch?"

"What other choice do you have, Nique. I think you are stuck with either having the surgery now or wait until it's almost too late."

"Yeah, you're right. We probably need to get a second opinion."

"Isn't he the second opinion?"

"Well, he's the pediatric specialist," Monique confirmed.

"Then what's to worry about?"

"I'm starting to think that he is just experimenting with my child."

"For what?"

"Bragging rights, or because a case like this is so rare. Not only do you have an infant with PKD, a rare genetic disease in children, but you also have an infant sibling as a donor. This is one for the books."

"I hate to be grim, but I think trying this surgery now will only help. At least if this doesn't work then you'll have time for something else. Right?"

"Not if Kalil's body rejects the kidney right away."

"So Yvonne is really going to go through with the surgery?"

"I'm almost positive. She stormed out of the office today before we could finish our consult," Monique laughed.

"You find that funny?" Alicia was disgusted.

"Don't get all brand new on me," Monique waved her off.

"You did help put the lady in this mess."

"She's just learning how to share."

"Nique you are sick," Alicia walked away from her. It was hard to give Monique any type of sympathy acting like that. Alicia knew that her friend had it bad. It was bad enough that she had taken away Yvonne's trust, she would not stop until she had Yvonne's life.

Yvonne took it upon herself to seek medical counsel on her own. When Dr. Anderson saw her coming, he figured this was just another episode in the soap opera. Yvonne asked him point blank, what he thought she, as a mother, should do. He told her to put herself in Monique's shoes. Excluding all of the personal mayhem that had transpired, what would she want someone to do for her child? Yvonne had her answer. She apologized to him for storming out during the last visit.

He told her that he understood what she was going through and that this was a very trying time in her life. She explained to him that Victor's concern was more for his other child and she was hurt by that. Dr. Anderson told her that he had both children's interest at heart and he would try his best to make sure they both got the care that they deserved.

Yvonne left Dr. Anderson's office armed with more information, yet displaying a heavy heart. Her attitude was not very optimistic. She knew deep down that what she was doing was the right thing to do. When it was all said and done, she needed to be able to sleep better at night knowing that she did all she could to save that innocent boy's life.

There were two people in the house, Yvonne and Kalia. Yvonne picked up her daughter and held her out on her lap. They were facing each other. Yvonne just looked at her. Kalia laughed and moved around, excited by the attention.

"You are about to do something that is very admirable." Yvonne spoke to the child. "I know you are Mommy's brave little girl. You have to do this for me. I don't know what your father was thinking when he put us in this position. He probably does not know himself."

"Loo," Kalia gurgled in response.

"Together Baby, we are going to get through this. Kalil is your brother. You are going to save his life. Stay healthy for Mommy. I love you." Yvonne hugged her child. She took a deep breath. The very scent of her daughter bought her to tears. Everything was just so overwhelming.

The surgery date came and all three parents were extremely anxious. They were all pulling for Kalil, praying that he would make it out okay. The waiting room was tense with all of them sitting there. Verbal language was at a minimum, but their bodies said it all. Monique was pacing the hallway, back and forth. Victor was sitting down, but he could not keep still. He was fidgeting and readjusting every 5 minutes. Yvonne was balled up with her feet in the chair and her arms crossed.

Dr. Anderson met up with them in the waiting room after what seemed like an entire lifetime. Both infants came out of surgery just fine and they were in recovery. For the next three days, the hospital staff kept a close watch on the siblings. Monique and Yvonne practically lived next to their children's gurneys. It was apparent that there was no love lost between the two. Victor came to the hospital and spent equal amounts of time with both children.

Yvonne felt bad for subjecting her daughter to the surgery. Seeing the tubes running into Kalia's tiny nostrils and wires attached to her short torso made Yvonne ache. Kalia seemed to be in pretty good spirits for having just gone through the procedure. Her recovery was coming along just fine. Dr. Anderson told Yvonne that she had a real trooper in Kalia. Yvonne commented that she was going to have to be, given the situation her father put her in.

Monique only left Kalil's side to use the bathroom or eat. Other than that, she was right there where he needed her to be. She was willing him back to health, praying earnestly for his full and total recovery. She was more than grateful to Yvonne.

When Monique originally heard that the donor match results came back, she called Yvonne herself to thank her. Yvonne told her the testing was not done for her and terminated the conversation. At the final consultation prior to the surgery, Monique again thanked Yvonne to which Yvonne just shook her head. In the waiting room, Monique again expressed how thankful she was that her child was going to be afforded the opportunity to live. Yvonne walked out of the room.

For the next hour, she wandered around the hospital. She was so unmoved by Monique's theatrics. Even worse was Victor. She expected Victor to be the one going over and beyond with thank you's. She settled that he knew she would do the right thing, a side from the fact that he felt guilty for even having to say thank you given the circumstances.

Watching her husband hold another woman's baby, it became clear to Yvonne that she would never be able to forgive Victor, nor live with the choice that he made to tip out on her. Yvonne was looking to protect her interests, her daughter and her heart. The day that Kalia was released from the hospital, Richard Worthy met Victor at the hospital to serve him with divorce papers. It was their anniversary.

Victor was furious. Yvonne knew how he felt about Worthy, although not the real reasons why. Here, years after his initial fall out with Worthy, Worthy finally got the answers he was looking for. It was really none of his business, but he knew the truth anyway.

As if having 2 families and a sick child were not enough, now Victor would also have to hear about his drama at work. Worthy would not miss the opportunity to make Victor's professional life a living hell. Victor could envision his former buddy standing in the break room at the office with a smirk on his face talking about his latest case…Victor and Yvonne Russell.

She searched her soul for a future with Victor. The more she tried to picture herself living a life with him, the more often she cried. Yvonne knew there was no way that she could look at Victor and believe anything he told her. Staying late to work, going to Sparky's, it was all the same to her, lies.

Monique tried to console him, but Victor was beside himself. The very life that he worked so hard to preserve was being stripped away from him. The only real family he had ever known, he destroyed with his own two hands. He looked at Monique and in his heart, he blamed her. All of it could have been prevented.

She told him that Yvonne was not a strong enough woman and that now he could have a real woman by his side. Monique followed him from the nursery to a waiting room down the hall.

"Victor everything I did, I did for you, for us."

"What do you mean everything you did?"

"I had this baby for you." She rubbed his head.

"Monique I asked you not to have the baby."

"I know, but I knew that you didn't mean it. You would have never forgiven yourself if I had done that." Victor pulled her hand away from him and slowly turned to look at her.

"What are you saying?"

"I was the one who called your office that day. I knew that you were in court and Ms. Betsy was going to call Yvonne and tell her that there was a message from the hospital. I was hoping she could piece two and two together then."

"What?"

"Yvonne is a fool. Even after I put the proof in her face, she still could not figure it out."

"Monique..." Victor looked at her with strange eyes. He could not believe the words that were coming out of this woman's mouth.

"You didn't want to tell her about us and I knew that she was going to find out eventually. I was just trying to move the process along." He had a blank look on his face. She really had been trying to set him up the whole time.

"You set me up?"

"You did it to yourself. Look we have a beautiful son together."

"Whatever plans you have for me and my life," Victor said pointing to himself, "you can flush them down the drain." He stood up and left.

"Victor...Victor!" She called out behind him. He was walking down the hall. Monique smiled because she knew he would be back. After all, she was his family too.

Carla F. Du Pont was born in West Palm Beach, FL. She now resides in the metro-Atlanta area.

www.bluecafebooks.com